ASHTAKAVARGA SYSTEM OF PREDICTION

BANGALORE VENKATA RAMAN

Editor : THE ASTROLOGICAL MAGAZINE

UBSPD

UBS Publishers' Distributors Ltd.

New Delhi Bombay Bangalore Madras

Calcutta Patna Kanpur London

UBS Publishers' Distributors Ltd.

5 Ansari Road, New Delhi-110 002
Phones: 3273601, 3266646 ☆ *Cable* : ALLBOOKS ☆
Fax : (91) 11-327-6593
e-mail: ubspd.del@smy.sprintrpg.ems.vsnl.net.in
Internet: www.ubspd.com

Apeejay Chambers, 5 Wallace Street, Mumbai-400 001
Phones : 2076971, 2077700 ☆ *Cable* : UBSIPUB ☆ *Fax* : 2070827

10 First Main Road, Gandhi Nagar, Bangalore-560 009
Phones : 2263901, 2263902, 2253903 ☆ *Cable* : ALLBOOKS ☆
Fax : 2263904

6, Sivaganga Road, Nungambakkam, Chennai-600 034
Phone : 8276355, 8270189 ☆ *Cable* : UBSIPUB ☆ *Fax* : 8278920

8/1-B, Chowringhee Lane, Calcutta-700 016
Phones : 2441821, 2442910, 2449473 ☆ *Cable* : UBSIPUBS ☆
Fax : 2450027

5 A, Rajendra Nagar, Patna-800 016
Phones : 672856, 673973, 656170 ☆ *Cable* : UBSPUB ☆
Fax : 656169

80, Noronha Road, Cantonment, Kanpur-208 004
Phones : 369124, 362665, 357488 ☆ *Fax* : 315122

Eighth Edition	1992
First Reprint	1993
Second Reprint	1993
Third Reprint	1994
Fourth Reprint	1996
Fifth Reprint	1997
Sixth Reprint	1998

Printed at Shivam Offset, New Delhi

CONTENTS

PREFACE TO THE EIGHTH EDITION

ı this eighth edition many of the charts have been reworked to ensure reater accuracy.

is hoped that this book will provide the astrological public with a basis ɪr research in the Ashtakavarga system of prediction, a unique aspect f Hindu Astrology.

he educated public have always welcomed my humble writings on strology and I solicit their continued support. They are my best judges ıd critics.

am thankful to UBS Publishers' Distributors Ltd., New Delhi, for ıving brought out this attractive edition.

B. V. RAMAN

angalore
2.1992

PREFACE TO THE FIRST EDITION

In these days of superfluous journalism and book-publication, any reflective person who contemplates writing a book on astrology must know his motive for doing so. Otherwise an infliction of oneself on the public calls for some apologetic explanation. For some time past there has been a persistent demand from a large section of my readers for a book that deals exclusively with Ashtakavarga, and the present work is intended to fulfil this demand.

I have been a student of astrology for nearly 35 years and have experimented in my own humble way with various methods of interpretation of horoscopes, mainly derived from ancient classical sources. The Ashtakavarga System, an exposition of which has been attempted in this book, has engaged my attention for a long time. It occupies an important place in the general scheme of Hindu astrology and offers considerable scope for an astrological student who has a scientific bent of mind for making further researches, especially in the matter of timing events. A large number of horoscopes taken out of my vast collections have been studied in the light of Ashtakavarga and a few important discoveries have also been made.

In regard to certain aspects of the system, such as whether the Ashtakavargas of Rahu and Lagna are to be considered, and whether the Ashtakavarga is to be reckoned on the basis of Rasis or Bhavas, there is difference of opinion even amongst ancient writers.

Such controversial matters have been avoided so that the astrological student may not get confused in understanding the main principles of the system. It is my humble view, and I have the support of noted classical writers, that the Ashtakavarga reckoning has to be done on the basis of the Rasis and not Bhavas.

Consistent with recognisable limitations and deficiencies on my own part, I have endeavoured to present in this volume a clear and concise exposition of the Ashtakavarga method in the hope that the exposition will stimulate the readers to pursue the subject in greater detail. In the treatment of the subject there is no strict adherence to traditional methods. Some minor departures have been made in the light of experience gained all these years.

I hope that this book will receive, from the educated public, the same favourable reception that has been extended to my other writings all these years.

18-6-1962 **B. V. RAMAN**

CHAPTER I

General Introduction

THE UNIQUENESS of Hindu astrology consists in the variety of methods employed for making predictions. Whether it is the Dasa system, Gochara or Ashtakavarga, there is a certain originality peculiar to Indian genius not to be found either in the Chaldean or the Ptolemaic or the modern western system. The Ashtakavarga method of prediction, an exposition of which is attempted in this treatise, has been quite popular with the rank and file of Hindu astrologers. But as usual, the method is so indiscriminately employed that its practical utility is often lost sight of. Most astrological practitioners of the traditional type in India generally wind up their horoscope readings by determining longevity (Ayurdaya) according to Ashtakavarga. Their confidence in the infallibility of the Ayurdaya system according to Ashtakavarga is so great that they hardly bother to verify the results.

In the interpretation of Dasas, a comprehensive knowledge of the various principles is no doubt essential. But a correct reading of the effects is always a matter of individual skill. Similarly in interpreting a horoscope according to Ashtakavarga, the astrologer, in addition to possessing a thorough knowledge of the rules should also be capable of interpretative skill which again is something purely individualistic.

As the famous work *Horamakaranda* says, as a result of the progression of the seven planets from their respective radical places and from Lagna, a collective factor sets in going under the name of Ashtakavarga. It is likely that a planet, say for instance the Sun, as a result of his horoscopic position in a particular sign, is capable of throwing out beams of influence on certain places declared as favourable, both from his position and from the positions of other planets, so that, such beams of influence contributed by different planets may act as a catalytic agent augmenting the good effects of radical as well as transit influences.

Ashtakavarga also takes into cognisance the actions and interactions of the transiting planets with regard to their radical situations (including the Lagna) and by a certain manipulation of the benefic and malefic influences given rise to by such movements and measured numerically as so many units—certain important events are determined.

When we say Sun's Ashtakavarga, we mean the collective factor due to the projection of positive beams with reference to himself and the other six planets and the Lagna. It is not my intention to discuss in this book the rationale of the Ashtakavarga system. The sages seem to have devised a numerical scheme of interpretation and timing of events, which is at once unique and capable of further development. I only propose to give a clear picture of the method as understood by me. Readers with a scientific bent of mind can certainly probe into the significance of the theory. In my humble experience of nearly thirty years in this field, I have found Ashtakavarga to be highly useful in making predictions. But so far as the determination of longevity is concerned, the Ashtakavarga system, it occurs to me, cannot be solely relied upon for accuracy. Hundreds of horoscopes have been worked out by me and in the majority of cases, longevity obtained on this basis is quite at variance from the actual number of years lived by the natives. The causes for the failure of Ashtakavarga may be due to either an inadequate comprehension of the principles or the inadequacy of the number of examples worked out. Readers will do well to study the following principles carefully, work out as many examples as possible and test for themselves the soundness or otherwise of my own inferences.

In regard to the predictive utility of Ashtakavarga, classical authors have expressed different opinions. However, by a careful study of the various books bearing on this subject, we find that the Ashtakavarga is employed for :

(*a*) Predicting the general strength of planets and houses (Bhavas),

(*b*) anticipating certain important life events,

(*c*) forecasting transit results, and

(*d*) determining longevity or Ayurdaya.

Planets occupy Bhavas. The relative strengths of Bhavas can no doubt be found numerically according to Sripathi and Kesava Paddhati involving laborious calculations. The Ashtakavarga, on the other hand, dispenses with cumbersome methods and enables us to attempt some sort of a snap-shot assessment of the strength of a Bhava. Thus if Mars is in Lagna (ascendant) and the sign which has reference to the ascendant has obtained a certain optimum number of benefic points in the Ashtakavarga of Mars, the Lagna becomes strengthened and capable of producing good results. Ashtakavarga essentially aims at a generalised assessment of vitality of a horoscope and therefore has its own limitations. Thus if Venus i in the second house; which has reference to Taurus, and in the Ashtakavarga of Venus, the benefic points number 7, or 8, the Venus becomes fully capable of conferring the maximum results due to his location as well as lordship.

In order to explain the Ashtakavarga principles we shall take the horoscope of a person born on 16th October 1918 at 2 p.m. (L.M.T.) at Bangalore, which for the sake of convenience, we shall call as the Standard Horoscope. The following are the planetary, Rasi and Navamsa positions :—

The Sun	....	179°	8′
The Moon	....	311	40
Mars	....	229	49
Mercury	....	180	33
Jupiter	....	83	35
Venus	....	170	4
Saturn	....	124	51
Rahu	....	233	23
Ketu	....	53	23
Lagna	....	294	57
Tenth House	....	214	55

		Ketu	Jupit.
Moon	RASI		
Lagna			Sat.
	Mars Rahu	Merc.	Sun Venus

		Jupit. Sat.	
Rahu	NAVAMSA		Venus
Moon			Lagna Ketu
Mars		Merc.	Sun

CHAPTER II

Ashtakavarga Charts

In this chapter, we shall give the details of casting the various Ashtakavarga charts. Broadly they can be classified thus :—

(1) Bhinnashtakavarga or individual Ashtakavarga charts ;
(2) Bhinnashtakavarga after reduction ;
(3) Sarvashtakavarga or total Ashtakavarga chart ; and
(4) Prasthara or spread-out Ashtakavarga chart.

Bhinnashtakavarga

The Sun :—The Sun's benefic places are the 1st, 2nd, 4th, 7th, 8th, 9th, 10th and 11th from himself ; the same places from Mars and Saturn the 5th, 6th, 9th and 11th from Jupiter ; the 3rd, 6th, 10th and 11th from the Moon ; the 3rd, 5th, 6th, 9th, 10th, 11th and 12th from Mercury; the 3rd, 4th, 6th, 10th, 11th and 12th from the Ascendant ; and the 6th, 7th and 12th from Venus. Total 48 points.

The Moon :—The benefic places of the Moon are the 3rd, 6th, 10th and 11th houses from the

Ascendant. The Moon is auspicious in the 2nd, 3rd, 5th, 6th, 9th, 10th and 11th houses from Mars; the 1st, 3rd, 6th, 7th, 10th and 11th houses from the Moon herself; the 3rd, 6th, 7th, 8th, 10th and 11th from the Sun; the 3rd, 5th, 6th and 11th from Saturn; the 1st, 3rd, 4th, 5th, 7th, 8th, 10th and 11th from Mercury; the 1st, 4th, 7th, 8th, 10th, 11th and 12th from Jupiter; and the 3rd, 4th, 5th, 7th, 9th, 10th and 11th from Venus. Total 49 points.

Mars :—The benefic places of Mars will be the 3rd, 5th, 6th, 10th and 11th houses from the Sun; the 1st, 3rd, 6th, 10th and 11th from the Ascendant; the 3rd, 6th and 11th from the Moon; the 1st, 2nd, 4th, 7th, 8th, 10th and 11th from himself; in 1, 4, 7, 8, 9, 10 and 11 from Saturn; in 3, 5, 6 and 11 from Mercury; in 6, 8, 11 and 12 from Venus; and in 6, 10, 11 and 12 from Jupiter. Total 39 points.

Mercury :—Mercury produces good in 1, 2, 3, 4, 5, 8, 9 and 11 from Venus; 1, 2, 4, 7, 8, 9, 10 and 11 from Mars and Saturn; in 6, 8, 11 and 12 from Jupiter; in 5, 6, 9, 11 and 12 from the Sun; in 1, 3, 5, 6, 9, 10, 11 and 12 from himself; in 2, 4, 6, 8, 10 and 11 from the Moon; and in 1, 2, 4, 6, 8, 10 and 11 from the Ascendant. Total 54 points.

Jupiter :—Jupiter will be auspicious in 1, 2, 4, 7, 8, 10 and 11 from Mars; in 1, 2, 3, 4, 7, 8,

10 and 11 from himself; in 1, 2, 3, 4, 7, 8, 9, 10 and 11 from the Sun; in 2, 5, 6, 9, 10 and 11 from Venus; in 2, 5, 7, 9 and 11 from the Moon; in 3, 5, 6 and 12 from Saturn; in 1, 2, 4, 5, 6, 9, 10 and 11 from Mercury; and in 1, 2, 4, 5, 6, 7, 9, 10 and 11 from the Ascendant. Total 56 points.

Venus :—Venus produces good in 1, 2, 3, 4, 5, 8, 9 and 11 from Lagna; in 1, 2, 3, 4, 5, 8, 9, 11 and 12 from the Moon; in 1, 2, 3, 4, 5, 8, 9, 10 and 11 from himself; in 3, 4, 5, 8, 9, 10 and 11 from Saturn; in 8, 11 and 12 from the Sun; in 5, 8, 9, 10 and 11 from Jupiter; in 3, 5, 6, 9 and 11 from Mercury; and in 3, 5, 6, 9, 11 and 12 from Mars. Total 52 points.

Saturn :—Saturn is beneficial in 3, 5, 6 and 11 from himself; in 3, 5, 6, 10, 11 and 12 from Mars; in 1, 2, 4, 7, 8, 10 and 11 from the Sun; in 1, 3, 4, 6, 10 and 11 from the Ascendant; in 6, 8, 9, 10, 11 and 12 from Mercury; in 3, 6 and 11 from the Moon; in 6, 11 and 12 from Venus; and in 5, 6, 11 and 12 from Jupiter. Total 39 points.

The total individual contribution of benefic points by any planet in any horoscope will be the same respective figures as given above. The sum total of benefic points of all planets will be 337 for any horoscope. This is constant.

In the Standard Horoscope, the Sun is in Kanya or Virgo. Therefore his benefic places from himself (in his own Ashtakavarga) will be Virgo (1st), Libra (2nd), Sagittarius (4th), Pisces (7th), Aries (8th), Taurus (9th), Gemini (10th) and Cancer (11th). This can be represented diagrammatically as per Chart No. 1. It is the practice to mark the benefic place by a *bindu* or zero (0) and the malefic place by a *rekha* or horizontal stroke (—).

0	0	0	0
—	Chart No. 1 Sun's Ashtaka- varga from Sun		0
—			—
0	—	0	0 Sun

Again in the Standard Horoscope, Mars is in Scorpio. Therefore in the Sun's Ashtakavarga, the benefic places from Mars happen to be Scorpio (1st), Sagittarius (2nd), Aquarius (4th), Taurus (7th), Gemini (8th), Cancer (9th), Leo (10th) and Virgo (11th). Charts 2 to 8 are diagrammatic representations of Sun's Ashtakavarga, with reference to Mars, Moon, Mercury, Jupiter, Venus, Saturn and Lagna.

—	—	0	0
0	Chart No. 2 Sun's Ashtaka- varga from Mars		0
—			0
0	0 Mars	—	0

—	0	—	—
Moon	Chart No. 3 Sun's Ashtaka- varga from Moon		0
—			—
0	0	—	—

0	—	—	0
0	Chart No. 4 Sun's Ashtaka- varga from Mercury		0
—			0
0	—	Merc.	0

—	0	—	Jupit.
0	Chart No. 5 Sun's Ashtaka- varga from Jupiter		—
—			—
—	0	0	—

0	—	—	—
0	Chart No. 6 Sun's Ashtaka- varga from Venus		—
—			0
—	—	—	Venus

0	0	0	0
0	Chart No. 7 Sun's Ashtaka- varga from Saturn		—
—			Sat. 0
—	0	—	0

0	0	—	0
—	Chart No. 8 Sun's Ashtaka-varga from Ascendant		—
Lagna			—
0	0	0	—

All the 8 charts pertaining to a planet can be reduced to a single diagram (Chart No. 9). By adding together all zeroes or bindus in Aries in each chart pertaining to the planet concerned, we shall get a number representing the total number of bindus in Aries. Similarly other signs have to be dealt with.

In the Standard Horoscope, the combined or collective Ashtakavargas of the Sun and other

5	5	3	5
5	Chart No. 9 Sun's Ashtakavarga-48		4
0			4
5	5	3	4 Sun

5	5	3	5
3 Moon	Chart No. 10 Moon's Ashtakavarga-49		5
5			3
6	4	3	2

4	4	3	4
5	Chart No. 11 Mars' Ashtakavarga-39		3
2			4
3	5 Mars	1	1

3	4	6	4
5	Chart No. 12 Mercury's Ashtakavarga-54		5
4			5
4	6	3 Mercury	5

4	3	4	7 Jupit.
4	Chart No. 13 Jupiter's Ashtakavarga-56		6
5			4
5	4	6	4

6	7	4	4
4	Chart No. 14 Venus' Ashtakavarga-52		3
5			3
4	3	5	4 Venus

4	5	2	4
1	Chart No. 15 Saturn's Ashtakavarga-39		4
3			3 Saturn
3	2	5	3

planets (Charts 9 to 15) can be represented thus: The total bindus in each sign can be put in figures instead of in zeroes.

Sarvashtakavarga

In casting the Sarvashtakavarga chart, Ashtakavargas of all the planets are considered. Add together the bindus contained in the sign Aries in each diagram. The aggregate will be the figure in the sign Aries in Sarvashtakavarga. Similarly the aggregate of the bindus in Taurus and other signs should be obtained. The addition should be carried out before applying the two reductions explained below.

In the Standard Horoscope, the total of the bindus in Aries in the Bhinnashtakavargas (Charts 9 to 15) of the different planets is 33.(Sun's Ashtakavarga 5+ Moon's 5+ Mars' 4+ Mercury's

31	33	25	33
27	Chart No. 16 Sarvashtakavarga of Standard Horoscope-337		30
24			26
30	29	26	23

4+Jupiter's 3+Venus' 7+Saturn's 5—total 33.) In a similar manner, figures in the different signs in the Sarvashtakavarga should be obtained.

If the calculations are correctly done, the total bindus of all the twelve signs in the Sarvashtakavarga will found to be 337.

Reductions

The figures in the Bhinnashtakavarga of each planet (Charts 9 to 15) are subjected to two types of reductions, *viz.*, Trikona and Ekadhipatya. These reduced figures are made use of both for the purpose of longevity determination and for making certain predictions in the birth horoscope. First the Trikona reduction is carried out and then the corrected figures are further reduced by the Ekadhipatya process.

Trikona Reduction

In a horoscope, there are four groups of Trikona Rasis (trinal signs), *viz*., (1) Aries, Leo and Sagittarius; (2) Taurus and its trines Virgo and Capricorn ; (3) Gemini, Libra and Aquarius and (4) Cancer, Scorpio and Pisces: (*a*) When the same number of bindus or figures is not found in a trinal group(*e.g.*, Aries, Leo and Sagittarius), subtract the least of the three figures from all the three and retain the remainders.(*b*) No reduction is called for if there is no figure in one of the signs of the group. (*c*) If there are no figures in two of the signs, then the figure in the 3rd must also be eliminated. (*d*) If the figures in the three signs of a group are equal, then all the figures in that entire group should be eliminated.

There is of course some difference of opinion amongst classical writers as regards the reduction or elimination of figures, but we have given the most approved method.

Taking the Sun's Ashtakavarga (Chart 9) in the Standard Horoscope : The figures in Aries, Leo and Sagittarius are respectively 5, 4 and 5. According to rule (*a*), subtract 4 (the least number) from each of the other two and the resulting numbers will be 1, 0, 1 respectively. Similarly in the second group of signs (Taurus, Virgo and Capricorn), the figures are 3, 4 and 0, Rule (*b*) is applicable and the reduced figures will be 3, 4 and 0 In the 3rd group of signs (Gemini,

1	1	3	2
2	Chart No. 17 Sun's Ashtakavarga after I Reduction		0
0			0
1	1	0	4

Libra and Aquarius) in the Sun's Ashtakavarga, the figures are 5, 3, 5. Here Rule (*a*) is applicable and the reduced numbers will be 2, 0, 2. After the I reduction, the Sun's Ashtakavarga will be as in chart in 17.

Thus the I reduction should be carried out for all the planets.

Ekadhipatya Reduction

The figures obtained from chart 17 after the I reduction will have to undergo a second reduction due to what is called Ekadhipatya or ownership of two signs by a single planet. Excepting Cancer and Leo, the other ten are Ekadhipatya signs. Therefore the second reduction for elimination of figures, obtained after the I reduction, is to be applied only to signs other than Cancer and Leo. The process involved is as follows :—

I. No reduction is called for (*a*) if there are planets in both the signs owned by a planet or (*b*) if there is no figure in one of the two signs, whether occupied or unoccupied.

II. If one of the two signs owned by the same planet is occupied and the other not, (*a*) if the figure in the former is greater than that in the latter, eliminate the latter ; (*b*) if the figure in the former is less than that in the latter, then make the latter equal to the former ; (*c*) if the figures in both the signs are equal, eliminate the figures in the latter.

III. If both the signs are not occupied, (*a*) if the figures in both or equal, eliminate both ; (*b*) if the figures are not equal, make the larger equal to the smaller.

Taking the Sun's Ashtakavarga in the Standard Horoscope :

Aries and Scorpio: One of the signs (Scorpio) is occupied by Mars and the other (Aries) not. Therefore eliminate the figures in Aries (II *c*).

Taurus and Libra : No figure in Libra and hence no reduction (I *b*).

Gemini and Virgo : No reduction because both the signs are occupied -- Gemini by Jupiter and Virgo by the Sun and Venus (I *a*).

Pisces and Sagittarius : Both the signs are not occupied and the figures are same. Therefore both the figures should be eliminated (III *a*).

0	0	3	2
2	Chart No. 18 Sun's Ashtakavarga after II Reduction		0
0			0
0	1	0	4 Sun

Capricorn and Aquarius : Capricorn has no figure. Therefore no reduction is called for (I *b*).

The Ashtakavarga of the Sun after II reduction (Ekadhipatya Sodhana) stands as follows :

After carrying out the I and II reductions, the Ashtakavarga figures, both before (B) and after (A) reductions, of all the planets can be represented as in Table I.

TABLE I

	Sun		Moon		Mars		Merc.		Jupit.		Venus		Sat.		Total	
	B	A	B	A	B	A	B	A	B	A	B	A	B	A	B	A
Aries	5	–	5	2	4	–	4	-	3	–	7	4	5	2	33	8
Taurus	3	3	3	1	3	2	6	2	4	–	4	–	2	–	25	8
Gemini	5	2	5	2	4	3	4	1	7	3	4	–	4	3	33	14
Cancer	4	–	5	1	3	–	5	2	6	2	3	–	4	2	30	7
Leo	4	–	3	–	4	1	5	1	4	1	3	–	3	–	26	3
Vigro	4	4	2	–	1	–	5	1	4	–	4	–	3	1	23	6
Libra	3	–	3	–	1	–	3	–	6	2	5	1	5	4	26	7
Scorpio	5	1	4	–	5	2	6	3	4	–	3	–	2	–	29	6
Sagittarius	5	–	6	1	3	–	4	–	5	2	4	1	3	–	30	4
Capricorn	–	–	5	3	2	1	4	–	5	1	5	1	3	1	24	7
Aquarius	5	2	3	–	5	4	5	2	4	–	4	-	1	–	27	8
Pisces	5	–	5	1	4	1	3	–	4	–	6	1	4	2	31	5

"B" means Before Reduction. "A" means After Reduction.

Mandala Sodhana

Expunge from figures in the different Rasis in the Sarvashtakavarga (Chart No. 16) multiples of 12. Then apply to the remaining bindus, the Trikona and Ekạdhipatya reductions and obtain the reduced Sarvashtakavarga.

Deducting multiples of 12 from the figures in the Standard Horoscope, we get the following corrected Sarvashtakavarga Chart :

7	9	1	9
3	Chart No. 19 Corrected Sarvashtakavarga		6
12			2
6	5	2	11

After applying the Trikona and Ekadhipatya reductions to the above the charts stand thus :

<table>
<tr><td>2</td><td>7</td><td>0</td><td>7</td></tr>
<tr><td>1</td><td colspan="2" rowspan="2">Chart No. 20
Sarvashtakavarga
after
I Reduction</td><td>1</td></tr>
<tr><td>11</td><td>0</td></tr>
<tr><td>4</td><td>0</td><td>0</td><td>10</td></tr>
</table>

<table>
<tr><td>2</td><td>7</td><td>0</td><td>7</td></tr>
<tr><td>1</td><td colspan="2" rowspan="2">Chart No. 21
Sarvashtakavarga
after
II Reduction</td><td>1</td></tr>
<tr><td>11</td><td>0</td></tr>
<tr><td>2</td><td>0</td><td>0</td><td>10</td></tr>
</table>

The use of these figures will be explained in later chapters.

Rekha Sarvashtakavarga

The total number of benefic and malefic points in a sign is always 56. Therefore if the bindus (benefic points) in a particular Rasi is subtracted from 56, the remainder represents *rekhas* or malefic units.

In the Sarvashtakavarga (Chart No. 16) of Standard Horoscope, take for instance Aries. It has 33 bindus. The number of Rekhas (malefic points) will be 56−33=23. The Rekha Chakras before (Chart No. 22) and after reductions (Charts 24 and 25) will be as follows :

25	23	31	23
29	Chart No. 22 Sarvashtakavarga (Rekhas)		26
32			30
26	27	30	33

1	11	7	11
5	Chart No. 23 Corrected Rekhas (Expunging multiples of 12)		2
8			6
2	3	6	9

0	9	0	6
0	Chart No. 24 Rekhas after I Reduction		1
1			4
0	2	1	2

0	2	0	6
0	Chart No. 25		1
1	Rekhas after II Reduction		4
0	2	1	2

Prasthara Ashtakavarga

We have hitherto learnt how to cast Bhinnashtakavargas of the different planets, the combined Astakavargas of all planets and the reduction of the bindus by the processes of Trikona and Ekadhipatya.

The next in importance is the diagrammatic representation of spreading-out of the benefic points (bindus) contributed or donated by each planet in respect of each Ashtakavarga. The benefic points (bindus) contributed by each of the planets are isolated so that while predicting Gochara or transit results or interpreting Dasas or analysing Bhavas the exact period or nature of effect can be clearly located. The tabular representation of the spreading-out or isolation of the benefic points, given out by each planet, is called 'Prasthara Chakra'.

According to classical writers, draw east to west 9 lines and north to south 13 lines and in this chakra (diagram) containing 96 houses, enter the points contributed by each planet (before reduction) in the descending order of Saturn, Jupiter, Mars, Sun, Venus, Mercury, the Moon and Lagna.

Table II on page No. 25 is the Prasthara Chakra of the Sun's Ashtakavarga in the Standard Horoscope :

The Sun is in Virgo. Therefore the spreading out starts from Virgo. In Table II, the bindus in the horizontal row against each planet indicate the auspicious places (in the Sun's Ashtakavarga) from the Sun and from other planets. The bindus in the vertical rows are those contributed by the different planets reckoned in the order of their orbits from the earth. For example the total figure in Virgo (in Sun's Bhinnashtakavarga) is 4 and these four bindus are contributed by Saturn, Mars, Sun and Mercury. The Moon, Jupiter, Venus and Lagna have not made any contribution. The Prasthara Chakras have to be prepared for each planet. The following are the Prasthara Chakras of the other planets in the Standard Horoscope :

TABLE II

SUN'S PRASTHARASHTAKAVARGA

	Virgo Venus Sun	Libra Mer-cury	Scorpio Mars	Sagit-tarius	Capri-corn Ascen-dant	Aqua-rius Moon	Pisces	Aries	Tau-rus	Gemini Jupiter	Can-cer	Leo Sa-turn	Total
Saturn	0		0.			0	0	0	0	0		0	8
Jupiter		0	0			0		0					4
Mars	0		0	0		0			0	0	0	0	8
Sun	0	0		0			0	0	0	0	0		8
Venus						0	0					0	3
Mercury	0			0		0	0			0	0	0	7
Moon			0	0				0			0		4
Ascendant		0	0	0			0	0		0			6
Total	4	3	5	5	0	5	5	5	3	5	4	4	48

TABLE III

MOON'S PRASTHARASHTAKAVARGA

	Moon Aquarius	Pisces	Aries	Taurus	Gemini Jupiter	Cancer	Leo Saturn	Virgo Sun Venus	Libra Mercury	Scorpio Mars	Sagittarius	Capricorn Ascdt.	Total
Saturn					0				0		0	0	4
Jupiter		0	0	0	0			0			0	0	7
Mars		0	0			0	0	0			0	0	7
Sun	0	0	0		0	0				0			6
Venus		0		0	0	0				0	0	0	7
Mercury	0		0	0		0	0		0		0	0	8
Moon	0		0			0	0			0	0		6
Ascendant		0			0				0	0			4
Total	3	5	5	3	5	5	3	2	3	4	6	5	49

TABLE IV

MARS' PRASTHARASHTAKAVARGA

	Scorpio Mars	Sagittarius	Capricorn Ascdt.	Aquarius Moon	Pisces	Aries	Taurus	Gemini Jupiter	Cancer	Leo Saturn	Virgo Sun Venus	Libra Mercury	Total
Saturn	0			0	0	0	0	0		0			7
Jupiter	0				0	0	0						4
Mars	0	0		0			0	0		0	0		7
Sun	0		0	0				0	0				5
Venus				0		0			0	0			4
Mercury		0		0	0					0			4
Moon		0				0			0				3
Ascendant	0		0		0			0				0	5
Total	5	3	2	5	4	4	3	4	3	4	1	1	39

TABLE V

MERCURY'S PRASTHARASHTAKAVARGA

	Libra Mercury	Scorpio Mars	Sagittarius	Capricorn Ascdt.	Aquarius Moon	Pisces	Aries	Taurus	Gemini Jupiter	Cancer	Leo Saturn	Virgo Sun Venus	Total
Saturn		0			0	0	0	0	0		0	0	8
Jupiter		0		0			0	0					4
Mars		0	0		0			0	0	0	0	0	8
Sun				0	0			0		0	0		5
Venus	0	0	0	0			0	0		0		0	8
Mercury	0		0		0	0			0	0	0	0	8
Moon		0	0			0		0		0		0	6
Ascendant	0	0		0	0		0		0		0		7
Total	3	6	4	4	5	3	4	6	4	5	5	5	54

TABLE VI

JUPITER'S PRASTHARASHTAKAVARGA

	Gemini Jupiter	Cancer	Leo Saturn	Virgo Venus Sun	Libra Mercury	Scorpio Mars	Sagittarius	Capricorn	Aquarius Moon	Pisces	Aries	Taurus	Total
Saturn		0			0		0	0					4
Jupiter	0	0	0	0			0	0		0	0		8
Mars	0		0	0		0	0		0			0	7
Sun	0	0		0	0	0	0			0	0	0	9
Venus	0	0			0			0	0			0	6
Mercury	0	0	0		0	0		0	0	0			8
Moon	0		0		0		0			0			5
Ascendant	0	0		0	0	0		0	0		0	0	9
Total	7	6	4	4	6	4	5	5	4	4	3	4	56

TABLE VII

VENUS' PRASTHARASHTAKAVARGA

	Virgo Venus Sun	Libra Mercury	Scorpio Mars	Sagittarius	Capricorn Ascdt.	Aquarius Moon	Pisces	Aries	Taurus	Gemini Jupiter	Cancer	Leo Saturn	Total
Saturn		0	0	0			0	0	0	0			7
Jupiter		0			0	0	0	0					5
Mars	0	0			0		0	0			0		6
Sun								0			0	0	3
Venus	0	0	0	0	0			0	0	0	0		9
Mercury				0		0	0			0		0	5
Moon	0	0		0	0	0	0	0	0	0			9
Ascendant	0		0		0	0	0	0	0			0	8
Total	4	5	3	4	5	4	6	7	4	4	3	3	52

TABLE VIII

SATURN'S PRASTHARASHTAKAVARGA

	Leo Sa- turn	Virgo Venus Sun	Libra Mer- cury	Scorpio Mars	Sagit- tarius	Capri- corn Ascdt.	Aqua- rius Moon	Pisces	Aries	Tau- rus	Gemini Jupiter	Can- cer	Total
Satarn			0		0	0					0		4
Jupiter			0	0					0	0			4
Mars	0	0	0			0		0	0				6
Sun		0	0		0			0	0		0	0	7
Venus	0						0					0	3
Mercury	0	0						0		0	0	0	6
Moon					0			0	0			0	3
Ascendant			0	0		0			0		0		6
Total	3	3	5	2	3	3	1	4	5	2	4	4	39

CHAPTER III

General Observations

Each chart has its own uses, which will become evident as the reader goes through subsequent pages. In the Ashtakavarga scheme, planets influence the houses they occupy in proportion to their own contribution of benefic influences to the Rasi in which they happen to be posited. Generally, a planet is said to become highly benefic if he secures in his own Ashtakavarga more than 5 bindus. A planet having less than 4 bindus will affect the bhava it is in, adversely. The results will generally be unfavourable indicating ill-health, wanderings, bad name, mental worry, anguish etc., the intensity being maximum when there is no bindu with the planet and gradually decreasing in proportion to the increase in the number of bindus. The results produced depend upon the bhava (house) which the planet occupies. Thus for example, if the bhava happens to be the 4th and the planet there has 1, 2 or 3 bindus, the person suffers misery in respect of all the events pertaining to the 4th bhava and also the events signified by the Karakatwa of the planet concerned. If the bhava is the 10th, the person's career will be marked by upsets in profession, loss of status and disappointments. If, on the other hand, the planet is associated with 5 or more bindus, it leads to the realisation of ambitions, acquisition of status, power and reputation. Even planets well placed in a chart; such as in exaltation etc., will lose their power to confer good results if they are not associated with the required number of bindus in their own Ashtakavargas.

It will be seen that the maximum number of bindus capable of being contributed by a planet is always eight.

Usually, matters to be looked into on the basis of Ashtakavarga pertain to those represented by the Karakatwas of planets as well as bhava indications.

From *the Sun* : should be ascertained spiritual matters, personal influence and father; from *the Moon*—intelligence and all that pertains to the mind and mother; *Mars*—lands, houses, brothers and sisters ; *Mercury*—power of discrimination, speech, sense of right and wrong and knowledge ; *Jupiter*—fame, conveyances, clothes, children, health, money, insignia of honour and fortune ; *Venus*—marriage, sense-pleasures, conveyances, female friends and features of the wife ; and *Saturn*—longevity, means of livelihood, sorrows, unhappiness, misery, destruction and accidental death.

The following are the significations of the various bhavas or houses :—

First House—The physical body and its features ; *second house*—fortune, finance and truth ; *third house*—vitality, prowess, brothers and sisters and voice ; *fourth house*—happiness, relations, residences and mother ; *fifth house*—nature, range of intelligence and issues ; *sixth house*—relatives, enemies and injuries ; *seventh house*—journeys and wife (and husband) ; *eighth house*—mental and physical ills, death and destruction ; *ninth house*—preceptor, general fortune and moral values (Dharma); *tenth house*—Karma or activity in general, means of livelihood, prowess, courage and fame ; *eleventh house*—wealth and gain of money ; and *twelfth house*—expenses, losses, sins, bodily destruction and moksha.

In interpreting the results due to the inherent indications (Karakatwa) of a planet or the signification of a house (bhava) one should pay due attention to the general principles of astrology. For instance bhavas occupied by malefics become weakened while those occupied by benefics become strengthened. As I have dealt with these details in my book *How to Judge a Horoscope*, I propose to confine myself here mainly to the Ashtakavarga system.

CHAPTER IV

The Sun's Ashtakavarga

The Sun gives the following results if he is associated with one or more bindus :—

1 Bindu : Various types of diseases, sorrows and aimless wanderings.

2 Bindus : Misunderstandings, anxiety due to rulers (or governments), displeasure and loss of money.

3 Bindus : The body gets emaciated due to frequent travels and the native will suffer from mental affliction.

4 Bindus : Parity of loss and gain and sorrow and happiness.

5 Bindus : Company of pious persons, birth of an issue, acquisition of new apparel, and educational attainments.

6 Bindus : Good health, physical charm and winning manners, acquisition of vehicles, decent fortune and good fame.

7 Bindus : High elevation, getting appropriate honours and riches.

8 Bindus : High political power or political honour and universal respect.

According to some authorities the above results generally happen when the Sun in his Ashtakavarga transits signs containing the different number of bindus. I have applied these principles to radical horoscopes also and have secured fairly satisfactory results in a number of cases. For instance, in a case where the Sun is in Cancer with 6 bindus in his own Ashtakavarga, the native is generally having good health, possesses vehicles, good fame and is fairly well-to-do financially. If the application is confined merely to transits, then whenever the Sun transits Cancer, the same effects must be recurring which is quite impracticable. I have also come across several cases where the Sun or a planet occupying his own sign but having very low bindus has adversely affected the bhava, which has reference to the Rasi in question. Therefore it occurs to me that one has to extend results ascribed to different planets having different bindus in their own Ashtakavargas, to matters other than mere Gochara transits.

1. If the Sun is in Lagna, debilitated or in an inimical place and the concerned Rasi has not more than three bindus, the native becomes sickly and will have a weak constitution. The evil effects are neutralised if possessing the same units, the Sun is exalted or occupies a friendly sign. On the other hand, if the Sun is exalted or

in a friendly place but has five bindus, the person will be long-lived, enjoying political power and eminence.

It cannot be a coincidence that in the horoscope of a noted Indian who held the high office of the head of state the Sun is in Lagna (Scorpio) in a friendly sign with five bindus. The native enjoyed great political power and was a capable administrator.

2. The person will always be ill if the bindus are 3 or 4 and the Sun does not happen to be in his place of exaltation or own sign.

3. One will be blessed with all the paraphernalia of political power and eminence if the Sun as ascendant lord is in a sign having more than 5 or 6 bindus.

In the horoscope of [2]Roosevelt the Sun, as lord of Lagna, is in Lagna, associated with 5 bindus. According to classical texts, such a disposition of the Sun clearly indicates long life and kingship (nrupatischirayu). *Naradeeya* is emphatic that when the Sun as lord of Lagna is associated with 5, 6 or 7 bindus, the native becomes a "King of many countries" (Bahubhumipala).

4. According to *Keraleeya*, the father gains political power 10 years after the birth of the native, if the Sun occupies a Kendra (the Rasi

having two bindus after reduction) in association with Saturn, Mars or Mercury.

5. The native's father may meet with death near a burial ground, or a mountain, or a fire-place, or sea if the sign occupied by the Sun has more than 5 bindus and happens to be a Kendra or Trikona.

6. The father expires in the 17th year of the native if the Sun is in a quadrant (Kendra) or a trine (Trikona) which should also be a friendly sign associated with 3, 4 or 5 bindus.

7. Death of the father happens after five years if the Sun is in the 9th with Rahu, and the number of bindus is 3.

8. The Sun in the 5th having 3 bindus, in association with Moon, Mars and Saturn destroys parents and brothers.

9. Death of the father takes place after the 20th year if the Sun is in the 3rd with 3 or 4 bindus aspected by malefics from the 9th.

10. When the Sun is in the 6th in a Rasi having 4 bindus, and aspected by Jupiter, father dies after the 25th year.

11. Death of the father will happen between 30th and 36th year of the native if the Sun is in a trine or angle and has five or more bindus.

The above combinations are interesting and reveal a certain apparent contradiction also. The positions allotted to the Sun are generally favourable in 6th, 11th, a trine or an angle. He is also further rendered strong by the association of the required minimum number of bindus. Yet adverse results are expected to happen. The strange thing is that in actual practice many of these dicta are found to hold good.

In the horoscope of a person born on 8th August 1912 A.D., at 7–35 p.m. (I S.T.) at Bangalore, the Sun is in Cancer in the 6th from Lagna aspected by Jupiter from Scorpio, having 6 bindus in his own Ashtakavarga. The father died in the 31st year of the native, *i.e.*, after the 25th year.

In several of the charts studied, it has been found that when the Sun is in an inimical place associated with the least number of bindus, the native died before the age of 40 ; when the Sun as 10th lord is in the 9th or 5th, associated with 5 or more bindus, legal eminence has been conferred ; in regard to Thula Lagna, the Sun's situation in an Upachaya has produced great intellectuality. These are just our observations and need not therefore be given the importance due to classical dicta.

12. Multiply the figure (before reduction) in the 9th from the Sun in Sun's Ashtakavarga by the *Sodya Pinda of the Sun. Divide the pro-

* The method of determining Sodya Pindas of planets has been explained in Chapter XIV.

duct by 27 and note the constellation that is arrived at by counting the remainder from Aswini (or from the star occupied by Saturn). When Saturn passes through this constellation (if the particular Dasa is inclined to effect maraka) death of father may take place. When Saturn passes through a star triangular to this, a near paternal relative may die.

In the Standard Horoscope: The Sodya Pinda of the Sun is 182. This, multiplied by the figure in the 9th (before reduction) from the Sun in his own Ashtakavarga, gives (182 × 3) = 546. This, divided by 27, leaves 6 as remainder. The 6th star from Aswini is Aridra. The 6th star from Makha (the asterism in which Saturn is placed in the birth horoscope) is Swathi. Therefore Saturn's transit of either of these two stars —whichever is more afflicted—may prove fatal to the father.

In regard to the case (birth: 8th August 1912) cited on page 41 the Sodya Pinda of the Sun is 157. The 9th from the Sun, in his own Ashtakavarga, has 5 bindus. Therefore the asterisms arrived at happen to be Bharani (2nd from Aswini) and Mrigasira (2nd from Rohini ,the star held by Saturn at birth). (157 × 5 = 785 ÷ 27 = remainder 2). The father of the native actually died when Saturn was transiting Mrigasira.

13. Multiply the total figures in the Sun's Ashtakavarga (after reductions) by the figures in the 9th from the Sun and divide the product by 27. The remainder counted from Aswini represents the star Saturn's transit of which may prove fatal to father.

In the Standard Horoscope: The total number of bindus (after reduction) in the Sun's Ashtakavarga is 12. The 9th from the Sun has 3 bindus. Therefore 12×3=36. Divide this by 27, the remainder will be 9. The 9th star from Aswini is Aslesha. When there is no figure in the 9th from Sun, then take the total number of bindus only. The maraka (death-inflicting) star should be fixed taking into consideration the term of longevity—short, middle or long—vouchsafed for the father.

14. Multiply the Sodya Pinda of the Sun by figures (before reduction) in the 7th from Jupiter in the Sun's Ashtakavarga. Divide the product by 27. The remainder counted from Aswini (or from the star held by Jupiter) may prove fatal to father when Jupiter transits it.

In the Standard Horoscope: The Sodya Pinda of the Sun is 182. This multiplied by 5 (the figure in the 7th from Jupiter in the Sun's Ashtakavarga) gives 910. The product, divided by 27, leaves a remainder of 19, which happens to be Moola. Jupiter's transit of this star may prove fatal to father's life. In regard to the 1912 case, the product of Sun's Sodya Pinda and the figure in the 7th from Jupiter is (157×5)=785. This, divided by 27, leaves a remainder of 2 and hence the fatal star for Jupiter to cause the death of the father will be Bharani.

15. The remainder obtained by dividing the product of the Sun's Sodya Pinda and the figure in the 7th from the Sun in his own Ashtakavarga (before reduction) by 27 represents the asterism the Sun's transit of which will prove fatal to the father.

In the Standard Horoscope the Sodya Pinda of the Sun is 182. This multiplied by 5 (the figure in the 7th from the Sun in the Sun's Ashtakavarga before reduction) gives 910. The product divided by 27 gives a remainder of 19. This will be Moola. When the Sun transits this star (15th December to 28th December) father's death can happen. In the 1912 case, the remainder is 2. Hence the Sun's transit of Bharani (the 2nd star from Aswini) or Makha (2nd from Aslesha, the star held by the Sun at birth) may cause the death of the father.

16. Multiply the figures in the 8th from the Sun in his own Ashtakavarga by the Sodya Pinda of the Sun. Divide the product by 12. The remainder counted from Aries will be the Rasi,

Saturn's transit of which may prove fatal to the native's life.

In the Standard Horoscope, the product of the Sodya Pinda of the Sun (182) and figures in the 8th (5) is 182×5=910. This divided by 12 leaves a remainder of 10. Hence Saturn's transit of Capricorn can prove fatal to the native.

17. Multiply the total figure in Sun's Ashtakavarga (after reductions) by the figure in the 8th from the Sun. The remainder obtained by dividing this product by 12, when counted from Aries, gives the sign through which or through one of its triangular ones, when the Sun passes, the native may die, After fixing the term of life, it is possible with the aid of Ashtakavarga to localise the year and month of death by noting the transits of certain fatal stars by Saturn, Jupiter and Sun.

CHAPTER V

The Moon's Ashtakavarga

In his own Ashtakavarga the Moon is said to give the following results due to his acquiring one or more bindus :—

1 Bindu : Fear from weapons and reptiles.
2 Bindus : Affliction to mother, sickness.
3 Bindus : Above results on a smaller scale.
4 Bindus : Prosperity to the house the person lives in.
5 Bindus : Mental peace, moral courage.
6 Bindus : Equanimity of mind, high ideals.
7 Bindus : Proficiency in Mantra Sastra.
8 Bindus : High moral courage and a happy and fortunate life.

1. If the Rasi occupied by the Moon is associated with 1, 2 or 3 bindus (in his own Ashtakavarga), the person suffers from distress, diseases, litigation and ill-health. In addition to this, if two or three planets join the Moon, the native is likely to pass away in his 37th year.

In the horoscope of Karl Marx, Moon as 6th lord is in the 3rd with only 2 bindus and is associated with Rahu. Marx is said to have runied his health by overwork. Havelock Ellis had the Moon (6th lord) weakly disposed in the 12th associated with only 3 bindus. The Moon is aspected by Saturn. He had to face heavy litigation due to his writings which were then considered obscene.

2. If the particular Bhava occupied by the Moon happens to be a Kendra, Trikona or the 11th and the Moon is debilitated or waning, and associated with 2 or 3 bindus, the Bhava in question will suffer annihilation.

The Moon in the 6th or 11th associated with more than 6 bindus is found to make one rich and when there is Jupiter's aspect, philanthropic also. In the horoscope of a dozen millionaires studied by me, the Moon was invariably in the 6th, 9th or 11th having 6 to 7 bindus. The lordship of the Moon seems to play an important part. As an instance I may refer to the case of Henry Ford. The Moon as lord of the 9th is in the 6th associated with 7 bindus. When the Moon is waxing even 5 bindus seem to make one fairly rich. Again in the horoscope of Duke of Windsor, the Moon (as lord of the 7th) is in the 11th, associated with 8 bindus and receiving the aspect of Jupiter. As a member of the British Royal family he was indeed rich. The lesser the number of bindus the Moon is with, the greater appear to be troubles from enemies.

The Moon as lord of the 5th or 9th and occupying places other than the 8th or 12th, appears to make one strong-minded, idealistic and philosophical. The late Sankaracharya of Govardhan Mutt has the Moon (as lord of 5th) in the 11th associated with 6 bindus.

3. The bhava in which the Moon is placed prospers in the course of the Dasa of the concerned lord, if the Moon is in a Kendra or Trikona associated with 5 or more bindus (after reduction).

4. One born when the Moon is in a Kendra and associated with 7 to 8 bindus, becomes highly learned, powerful, a ruler and endowed with wealth.

The Moon as lord of Lagna is in the 4th, associated with 6 bindus, and Jupiter is exalted in the 10th from the Moon, in the horoscope of His Highness Sri Krishnaraja Wadiyar of Mysore. He was noted for his equanimity of mind, intellectuality, philanthropy and idealism. He was of course a ruler endowed with riches.

5. Mother's death takes place after as many years as the number of bindus associated with the Moon occupying the 4th house. Early death to mother can be predicted if the waning Moon associated with no bindus occupies the 7th, 12th or 8th.

6. The mother suffers from frequent ill-health if Rahu is in the 2nd and the Moon occupies the 7th or 8th with 1, 2 or 3 bindus.

7. If Mars associated with less bindus is in the 4th or 8th from the Moon, then separation from mother takes place.

8. Mother's death is likely in the 36th year if the Moon occupies a kendra or the 12th with 1 to 3 bindus and the 4th house is joined by malefic planets.

9. The waning Moon in Lagna associated with 1, 2, 3 or no bindus indicates danger from weapons and poisonous insects ; there is also a likelihood of the mother's death.

10. Mother's death can take place in the 36th year if the 4th house is occupied by malefics and the Moon is in Lagna associated with few bindus.

11. The 4th from the Moon has reference to mother. Multiply the bindus in the 4th from the Moon (before reduction) by the Moon's Sodya Pinda. Divide the product by 27. When Saturn transits the constellation signified by the remainder, the mother's death takes place.

In the Standard Horoscope, the Sodya Pinda of the Moon is 100. The number of bindus in the 4th from the Moon is 3 (BR). The product of these two, *viz.*, 300 divided by 27 leaves 3 as remainder. This counted from Aswini gives the star as Krittika. Mother's death is likely when Saturn transits Krittika. According to some authorities the count could also be done from the star held by Saturn at birth. In the Standard Horoscope, Saturn is in Makha. The 3rd from this is Uttara.

12. By multiplying the Sodya Pinda of the Moon by the figures in the 7th from Jupiter and the 7th from the Sun and dividing the product severally by 27, the asterisms which will be transited by Jupiter and the Sun respectively, at the time of the mother's death, can be ascertained.

In the Standard Horoscope, the Moon's Sodya Pinda is 100.

(Jupiter): $(100 \times 6) \div 27 =$ Remainder 6, *i.e.* Aridra.

(Sun): $(100 \times 5) \div 27 =$ Remainder 14, *i.e.* Chitta.

Death of the mother is likely when Jupiter transits Aridra and the Sun Chitta (10th October to 24th October).

13. Multiply the total of the figures (after reduction) in the Moon's Ashtakavarga by the bindus in the 4th from the Moon. Divide the product by 27. Find the star obtained by counting the remainder from Aswini. When Saturn passes through this or its triangular ones, the person loses his mother.

In the Standard Horoscope, the total figure in the Moon's Ashtakavarga (after reduction) is 11 and the bindus in the 4th from the Moon is 1. $\therefore 11 \times 1 = 11 =$ Poorvaphalguni.

Saturn's transit of Bharani, Poorvaphalguni and Poorvashadha may prove critical to mother's life.

CHAPTER VI

Mars' Ashtakavarga

Mars indicates the following results if he is associated with one or more bindus in his own Ashtakavarga :

0 : Digestive troubles, epilepsy and fear of death.

1 Bindu : Bodily affliction, fever.

2 Bindus : Quarrels, separation from kith and kin.

3 Bindus : Separation from kith and kin.

4 Bindus : Equal proportion of good and bad.

5 Bindus : Charming behaviour, good conduct.

6 Bindus : Favours from rulers.

7 Bindus : Prosperity to brothers an benefits from them.

8 Bindus : Vanquishing of enemies, gai of land and wealth.

The Ashtakavarga of Mars is useful i assessing the number of brothers and sister their prosperity and adversity and acquisition landed property and wealth.

1. (*a*) Usually the number of the bindus (before reduction) in the 3rd from Mars in his own Ashtakavarga is said to denote the number of brothers and sisters one is likely to have. Bindus contributed by male and female planets represent the number of brothers and sisters respectively. The actual number surviving should be ascertained by eliminating the bindus donated by planets in debility and those occupying inimical places. (*b*) According to some authorities, the sum of the number of bindus in the 3rd from Mars and those associated with the 3rd lord (in Mars' Ashtakavarga) represents the number of brothers and sisters.

In actual practice both these rules seem to hold good. As to which should be applied depends upon the general disposition of the 3rd bhava.

In the Standard Horoscope, the 3rd from Mars (in his own Ashtakàvarga, Chart No. 11) has 2 bindus. But since the 3rd bhava is well disposed, Rule 1 (*b*) may be applied. According to this, bindus in 3rd from Mars and those with lord of the 3rd from Mars total 6, the contributors being Sun, Lagna, Saturn, Mars, Venus and Mercury (*see* Prasthara of Mars on page 27). Though Saturn is a "hermophrodite", he can be considered as a 'male' while Mercury can be considered as female. Venus (female) one of the contributors is debilitated. Hence we can infer that the total number of brothers and sisters born will be 6. Out of this, those that survive will be 4 males and 1 female.

2. When Mars is exalted or is in his own sign occupying the 9th, 4th, 10th or 1st house, associated with 8 bindus, the person becomes a millionaire.

3. One will become a ruler if Sagittarius, Leo, Aries, Cancer or Capricorn happens to be the ascendant and Mars occupies it, associated with 4 bindus.

4. Generally, if Mars has 8 bindus one rises to a high position such as head of a small principality.

In modern parlance, it means a high government official or even a minister, depending upon the strength or Mars.

5. If in addition to acquiring 8 bindus, Mars happens to be in the ascendant or the 10th or the 2nd, he will become a king or head of a government.

6. If in addition to these if Mars is also exalted or in his own house, the person becomes a powerful ruler.

7. One will become wealthy if Mars, associated with 4 or more bindus occupies the Lagna, Chandra Lagna, or the 9th or the 10th house

which should also happen to be his own or exaltation sign.

In the Standard Horoscope, Mars is in the 10th from the Moon, having 5 bindus (BR). Though born in a middle class family, the native became fairly rich.

8. Mars as lord of the 2nd in the 6th endowed with 6 bindus can confer on a person all the comforts of life but he will always have plenty of enemies to contend with.

9. One will be an adopted son if Mars, as lord of Lagna or the 8th, is in Lagna, or Chandra Lagna or in the 10th or 9th, associated with no or a few bindus and joined by a debilitated or inimical planet.

10. One will have no brothers if Mars with 6 bindus occupies the 6th, 8th or 12th being debilitated or combust and joined by waxing Moon.

Under the above combination if Mars is strong, one becomes a head of a town or a municipal corporator.

11. The same results accrue if Mars, possessing 4 bindus, occupies the 5th, Lagna, or a quadrant.

12. There will also be loss of brothers and sisters (by abortion to mother) if Mars or Saturn with 1 to 3 bindus occupy the 3rd house. If the lord of the 3rd or the lord of the sign occupied

by Karaka (Mars) is in an odd sign, brothers will die ; if it is an even sign, sisters will die.

13. No brothers or sisters will be born if the ascendant is a movable sign, and Saturn with 1 to 3 bindus occupies a common sign. If the ascendant is a common sign and Saturn is in a movable sign, similar results will happen. If the ascendant is a fixed sign and Saturn or Mars is associated with 1 to 3 bindus, there will be loss of father and brothers.

14. The ascendant being a movable sign and Saturn with 5 bindus is in a movable or fixed sign, one becomes not only wealthy but also possessed of brothers.

15. When the Lagna is a fixed sign and the 3rd lord is in a common sign with 5 bindus, the person will live long, enjoy all the pleasures of life and will possess a number of brothers.

16. One will have a number of brothers if Mars is in the 3rd with 5 or more bindus associated with or aspected by a benefic.

17. There will be loss of brothers when (*a*) Mars, devoid of bindus and joined by the lord of the 7th, is debilitated or combust or is in association with malefics, (*b*) when Mars and Saturn occupy Lagna, associated with 1 to 3 bindus, (*c*) when Mars endowed with 1 to 3 bindus is in the 8th from Saturn or *vice versa*, (*d*) when Mars is in the 8th from Saturn and

malefics are in the 3rd from Lagna, both with 1 to 3 bindus.

In the combination, the sign in which Mars is placed as well as the sign in which the malefics are placed should have 1 to 3 bindus.

18. According to *Keraleeya* (*a*) the number of brothers corresponds to the number of bindus present in the sign occupied by Mars, or its trines, whichever is aspected by a benefic planet.

Some commentators think that the total number of bindus in the sign occupied by Mars and its trines should be considered and then bindus in the sign or signs aspected by malefics should be deducted. It is my humble experience that the latter interpretation does not hold good in actual practice.

19. If Mars is in the 3rd associated with three bindus, the number of brothers will be 9.

20. When the 3rd house is associated with 3 bindus, the number of brothers will be equal to the number of navamsas gained by Mars.

The 3rd bhava should be carefully studied and its vitality assessed before applying the Ashtakavarga principles.

21. According to *Naradeeya* (*a*) the number of bindus in the sign occupied by Mars will represent the number of brothers and (*b*) those that will live long will correspond to the number of

bindus left in the sign occupied by Mars after the triangular reduction.

In several charts studied by us, Rule 21 (*a*) has been found to hold good while 21 (*b*) is not altogether reliable.

22. One becomes head of a state if Mars occupies Kendra or Trikona identical with Sagittarius, Aries or Capricorn associated with 4 bindus.

23. Similarly a person becomes head of a state if Mars with 5 bindus is in conjunction with or in mutual aspect with Saturn.

24. If, on the other hand, Mars with 1 to 3 bindus is in conjunction with or aspected by Mercury, poverty and sorrow will be the result.

25. One becomes head of two or three villages if Mars with 5 or more bindus joins or is aspected by the Moon.

26. A person becomes head of an army if Mars is in the 10th with 4 bindus aspected by Saturn. One born in a royal family can get command over fortresses if Mars occupies the 4th identical with his own sign and associated with 4 bindus. He becomes a commander-in-chief if in the above combination Mars occupies the 10th instead of the 4th. A Brahmin, a Vaisya and a Sudra born under the above combination will respectively perform many religious sacrifices, will become a great trader and a commander.

The combinations given above pertaining to Ashtakavarga of Mars are only some typical ones. It is possible to formulate fresh combinations to extend the scope of those to be found in classical texts by recourse to study of practical horoscopes. According to (10) one will have no brothers if Mars associated with 6 bindus occupies the 6th, 8th or 12th. It has been found that the 3rd and 11th house-disposition of Mars with more than 5 or 6 bindus is capable of giving rise to the same results. For example, [3]Mr. Jawaharlal Nehru has Mars in the 3rd associated with 6 bindus. He has no brothers. Mars, being Yogakaraka, aspects the 10th, endowed with 75% Ashtakavarga strength. As soon as Mars' Dasa commenced, Raja Yoga results were conferred. The horoscope of Roosevelt is another example of Mars, as Yogakaraka being invested with nearly 60% Ashakavarga strength. Here as Yogakaraka, Mars is in the 11th aspecting lord of Lagna and of 10th. Martian aspect on the 6th rendered Roosevelt sickly throughout life.

A noteworthy feature of [10]Mussolini's horoscope is that the Lagna or ascendant being a martian sign (Scorpio) is associated with 7 bindus while Mars in the 7th is endowed with 6 bindus. This made the native aggressive and violent. Combination (23) holds good *in toto* because Mars strengthened by more than 5 bindus, is in conjunction with Saturn enabling the native to become the head of state. He was indeed the supreme Dictator of Italy. Mr. Golwalkar, leader of the R.S.S., is the only surviving son, eight of his brothers and sisters having passed away. He has Mars in the 3rd with only 3 bindus. According to (12) such a disposition denotes loss of brothers and sisters.

27. Multiply the Sodya Pinda of Mars by the bindus in the 3rd from Mars (before reduction). Divide the product by 27. When Saturn transits the asterism signified by the remainder, brothers will die or suffer from affliction. Treat in the same way the Sodya Pinda of Mars with the bindus in the 7th from Jupiter and those in the 7th from the Sun severally. When Jupiter and the Sun pass through the asterisms so arrived at, evil will befall the brothers.

In the Standard Horoscope, Sodya Pinda of Mars is 197.

	Saturn	Jupiter	Sun
Therefore	197	197	197
	×2	×3	×4
	27) 394	27) 591	27) 788
	Remainder 16	Remainder 24	Remainder 5

The constellations revealed are Visakha, Satabhisha and Mrigasira. The brothers will suffer when Saturn transits Visakha, Jupiter

ransits Satabhisha and the Sun transits Mriga-
ira.

28. Multiply the Sodya Pinda of Mars by he number of bindus in the 3rd from him and livide the product by 12. When Jupiter transits he Rasi arrived at by counting the remainder rom Aries, the brothers will become prosperous and fortunate.

In the Standard Horoscope— 197
×2
394÷12

Remainder 10 Capricorn

When Jupiter transits Capricorn brothers will enjoy prosperity.

No hint is thrown as to how to find out which brother would become prosperous when one has more than one brother. We have to fall back on the horoscopes of the brothers and then combine the indications in their horoscopes with the indications in one's own chart or it is to be inferred that the period will be generally good for all brothers which seems improbable.

CHAPTER VII

Mercury's Ashtakavarga

When Mercury has one or more bindus in his Ashtakavarga, the following results are given rise to :—

0 : Fear of death and foes.
1 : Loss.
2 : Uneasiness due to misunderstandings with family members.
3 : Worry due to loss of wealth.
4 : Loss of occupation.
5 : Friendship and understanding with all.
6 : Success in understandings.
7 : Wealth, happiness and honour.
8 : Grace of rulers.

1. Family, wealth and children should be studied from the 4th house from Mercury. Spiritual attainments, learning, writing and intelligence should be ascertained from the 5th from Mercury.

2. If Mercury with 8 bindus occupies a quadrant or a trine, one becomes proficient in learning pertaining to his own caste or class. The prosperity of the bhava occupied by Mer-

cury in exaltation or own house and associated with 2 or 3 bindus is assured. Such a bhava will not suffer extinction.

3. When Mercury with 1 to 3 bindus is in the 6th or 8th devoid of benefic aspects, one becomes a hypocrite and crooked in outlook.

4. Associated with 1 to 3 bindus, if Mercury occupies the 6th, 8th or 12th in conjunction with Venus, one becomes uneducated.

5. When Mercury is in a trine or a quadrant associated with 5 bindus, and joined or aspected by Jupiter or Saturn, the person becomes highly learned in the Vedas.

6. Great proficiency in astrology is indicated if Mercury with 5 bindus is in the 4th or 6th from Saturn and Jupiter occupies or aspects the 2nd.

7. One becomes a great logician when Mercury, with 5 bindus conjoins Jupiter or is in association with or aspected by Mars.

8. If Ketu, associated with 3 bindus (in Mercury's Ashtakavarga) is in the 5th house or with the lord of the 5th house, one becomes an expert in astrology and allied subjects.

9. Disposition of Mercury with 4 bindus in a sign of Mars and in a Navamsa of Venus, aspected by Jupiter, makes one a litterateur.

10. Proficiency in dance, drama, music, mining and mesmerism can be predicted when

Mercury with 4 bindus is joined by malefics and is in debilitation in Navamsa.

11. According to sage Garga, a Bhava becomes defunct when Mercury occupies an even Navamsa with 1 to 3 bindus. Some writers opine that the Yugma Navamsa referred to by Garga implies the Navamsa of Gemini and not an even Navamsa.

12 Fame, intelligence and learning will be the consequence if the lord of the sign occupied by Mercury happens to be placed in a trine or quadrant associated with more bindus. If however, such a lord is in the 6th, 8th or 12th one will have break in education.

13. The Bhava occupied by Mercury prospers (*a*) provided Mercury is exalted or is in his own house having secured 1 to 3 bindus, (*b*) when Mercury is debilitated, occupies an inimical sign or is in combustion, having secured 4 or more bindus. Under (*b*) if the bindus are less than 4, the bhava cannot flourish satisfactorily.

In the Standard Horoscope, Mercury (Chart No. 12) is in a quadrant with 3 bindus aspected by Jupiter. Ketu is in the 5th associated with 6 bindus while combination (8) requires only 3 bindus. The native's Mercury's Dasa begins in 1964. She has immense interest in Vedic learning and Astrology and Mercury Dasa should therefore prove highly significant enabling her to attain good insight into these branches of knowledge. Venus, lord of the sign occupied by Mercury, is in the 9th with 5 bindus. Consequently, combination (12) bestows great intelligence on the subject.

14. When the 2nd from Mercury is devoid of bindus, the native will either be a mute or unable to express himself clearly.

15. If there are 2 or 3 bindus, the person's speech will be unsteady (*chapala vak*) or incoherent.

16. 4, 5 or 6 bindus make one a powerful and agreeable speaker and the words of such a person will carry weight.

17. 7 bindus in the 2nd from Mercury make one a great poet, while 8 bindus render one unassailable in speech. One will be vainglorious if the bindus of malefic planets predominate Otherwise he will talk moderately and with humility.

It will be seen that in the Standard Horoscope, the 2nd house from Mercury contains 6 bindus. The native is capable of clear, unambiguous and logical expression. 3 bindus are contributed by benefics.

18. If the bindu is contributed by the Sun, the native's speech will be patronising; if by Saturn obscure words are uttered or the native speaks mostly falsehood ; if by Mars, the speech

will be provocative and cruel; Mercury—pleasing and witty ; Jupiter—clear, intelligent and edifying; Venus—interspersed with anecdotes and ideals ; unafflicted Moon—frank and charming talk; and afflicted Moon—loose and careless talk.

19. If there are no bindus in the Rasi occupied by Mercury (after reduction) the native will be dispirited and lethargic.

20. Multiply Mercury's Sodya Pinda by the bindus (before reduction) in the 2nd from Mercury in his own Ashtakavarga and divide the product by 12. The remainder represents the Rasi (counted from Aries), the Dasa and the Bhukti of the lord of which confers benefic results pertaining to education, friends, arbitration etc. Similar results can be expected when Jupiter transits the said Rasi.

In the Standard Horoscope :

Sodya Pinda of Mercury × Bindus in 2nd.

158 × 6 = 948/12 = 79/0 or 12 Remainder = Pisces.

The period of Jupiter and the period when Jupiter transits Pisces should prove highly favourable to the native in respect of all the Karakatwas of Jupiter.

21. Multiply Mercury's Sodya Pinda by the bindus in the 4th from Mercury and divide the product by 27. When Saturn transits the

asterism indicated by the remainder, there will be misunderstandings with relatives, mental worry and general affliction.

In the Standard Horoscope :

Sodya Pinda of Mercury × Bindus in 4th :

158 × 4 = 632/27 = 23–11/27 = Pubba.

Saturn's transit of Pubba is adverse for the above events.

22. Multiply the Sodya Pinda by the figures in the 10th from Mercury and divide the product by 27. When Saturn transits the asterism indicated by the remainder, the native suffers from disappointments, loss in business or set-backs in career.

In the Standard Horoscope :

Sodya Pinda of Mercury × Bindus in 10th :

158 × 5 = 790/27 = 29–7/27 = Punarvasu.

When Saturn transits Punarvasu, loss in business and a generally adverse period may be expected.

Combination 12 is to be found in the horoscopes of several religious heads and saints. In the nativity of late [12]Sri Narasimha Bharati of Sringeri lord of the sign occupied by Mercury, viz., Saturn is in the 10th having 6 bindus. His spiritual and intellectual attainments were unrivalled. The late Sankaracharya of Govardhan Mutt has Mercury associated with 7 bindus in the 12th with Mars; but the lord of that sign, Saturn, is in the 9th with 6 bindus. He was a learned man and capable of discourses on different subjects. In the case of [13]Sri Ramana Maharshi, Mars lord of the sign occupied by Mercury is not only in his own house in the 7th but is associated with 5 bindus. His fame and spiritual attainments had won universal acclamation.

[14]Prof. B. Suryanarain Rao had not only attained great proficiency in astrology but had a deep knowledge of the Vedas. Mercury is in the 10th with 5 bindus joined by Jupiter and the 2nd from the ascendant is aspected by Jupiter.

CHAPTER VIII

Jupiter's Ashtakavarga

When Jupiter gets one or more bindus, the results will be as follow :—

0 Bindu : Loss of relatives and riches.
1 Bindu : Ill-health and affliction.
2 Bindus : Fear from rulers.
3 Bindus : Ear troubles, loss of energy.
4 Bindus : Not much good and not much evil.
5 Bindus : Destruction of enemies, success in all endeavours.
6 Bindus : Gain of riches, conveyances etc.
7 Bindus : Great fortune and happiness.
8 Bindus : Great fame, happiness and riches.

1. There will be acquisition of wealth, des-ruction of enemies and good longevity if Jupiter vith 5 or more bindus occupies the 6th, 8th or 2th.

In the Standard Horoscope, Jupiter is in the th associated with 7 bindus and the beneficial esults suggested above should hold good.

2. One becomes unfortunate having to ruggle in life if the Sun occupies a Rasi having

the last number of bindus in Jupiter's Ashtaka-varga.

3. When Jupiter, endowed with 8 bindus, is in a quadrant, a trine, in exaltation or own house, or in any other place free from combustion or unconnected with the planet's debilitation or inimical signs, the person becomes a ruler by dint of his own capacity.

This combination is very generally stated and is said to arise provided Jupiter has 8 bindus and does not occupy the sign of debilitation or of an enemy. Some scholars give it a different interpretation. Jupiter must be exalted, or occupy his own house, or be free from combustion, or should not be in an enemy's house. In addition, he should be in a kendra or trikona. I am inclined to think, on the basis of examination of number of charts, that in respect of each part of the combination, the intensity of the yoga must vary. Thus, exalted in a kendra with 8 bindus, the yoga will be powerful. Free from combustion and not disposed in the house of an enemy, but occupying a place other than a trine or a quadrant, Jupiter nevertheless causes the yoga, but the intensity is lessened. One should therefore be careful in assessing the importance of such yogas in actual practice.

4. In *Naradeeya*, another authoritative work, it is clearly stated that if Jupiter, associated

with 8 bindus, is in a kendra or a trikona identical with his exaltation or own sign, one becomes rich, a ruler or an equal to him. A Brahmin born under this yoga is said to become a *deekshita* or performer of sacrifices, owning villages, well-versed in sastras and respected in assèmblies. A Vaisya is said to become an expért trader, while a Sudra, who has this combination, will be a commander earning his livelihood by serving rulers.

We must remember that today we are living in an age in which the rigours of *Varnashrama Dharma* have been fast disappearing and that such combinations should be interpreted, taking into consideration, the society as it exists today and not as it existed when these principles were adumbrated.

5. If under the above combination, Jupiter has 7 bindus, the person will be endowed with riches, women and fortune; if with 6 bindus, one will have conveyances and wealth and if with 5 bindus, character and success.

[15]Dr. Rabindranath Tagore has Jupiter exalted in the 5th and associated with 7 bindus. Obviously the blessings of the combination were fully conferred on him. Even in the horoscope of [16]Stalin, Jupiter is in the 5th with 7 bindus. This is a powerful Raja Yoga.

6. Acquisition of wealth, victory over enemies and good longevity will be the consequences if Jupiter being associated with 5 or more bindus occupies the 6th, 8th or the 12th house.

This combination is totally applicable to the Standard Horoscope, as Jupiter is in the 6th and has secured 7 bindus. The native can be said to be highly fortunate in certain matters.

7. One will always be in debts and sorrow even though born under Raja Yoga combinations if the Moon with 1 to 3 bindus is in the 6th or 8th from Jupiter.

8. When the lord of the Rasi, occupied by Jupiter, is exalted or is in his own house, endowed with 5 or more bindus, one becomes prominent amongst rulers.

9. A person, born in Kesari Yoga, will be endowed with wealth and happiness, provided Jupiter occupies the Moon's Navamsa, with 5 or more bindus.

10. If the lord of the sign occupied by Jupiter is in the 6th or 8th from Jupiter, associated with 3 bindus, the person will be poor, or of moderate means.

11. If the lord of the sign occupied by Jupiter is disposed in a quadrant or a trine with 4 or more bindus in Jupiter's Ashtakavarga, the person becomes rich and fotunate in family life.

In the Standard Horoscope, Mercury, lord of the sign occupied by Jupiter, is in a quadrant having 6 bindus.

12. Jupiter with 1 to 3 bindus in debilitated Navamsa and Saturn in the 2nd or 11th make one a dunce.

13. If Jupiter with 4 or more bindus is in a kendra from Venus, as well as from Lagna, and if both Venus and Jupiter are in mutual association or aspect, one becomes a ruler or an equal to him.

14. One will have ordinary intelligence and become unlucky if the Lagna, associated with 1 to 3 bindus, happens to fall in the 6th or 8th from Jupiter and the lord of Lagna is weak.

15. If Jupiter or the lord of the 9th or 10th, associated with 7 or more bindus, is in a quadrant and the lord of the house occupied by either of the three is strong, the person becomes highly fortunate.

In the Standard Horoscope, Jupiter is associated with 7 bindus while Mercury lord of the 9th is associated with 6 bindus. The native can be said to be quite fortunate.

16. The father attains eminence through the son if the lord of the ascendant is in the 2nd or 9th and Jupiter endowed with 5 or more bindus occupies a quadrant.

17. If Jupiter, as lord of the 9th and associated with more bindus, occupies a kendra, or own or exaltation house, one becomes a ruler or commander-in-chief.

18. There will be sorrow through loss of children if Jupiter associated with 1 to 3 bindus occupies his own sign, which happens to be Lagna or a trikona, joined by malefic planets.

19. If the lords of the 5th and 8th interchange, and both the lords, devoid of bindus, are unaspected by Jupiter, there will be trouble from children and grandchildren.

20. There will be loss of as many children as there are bindus in the 3rd and 5th from Jupiter—provided Jupiter occupies the 6th, 8th or 12th from Lagna.

Here loss of children should not be predicted unless Jupiter is considerably afflicted.

21 A son who will be a beacon to the family will be born if the lord of the house, occupied by the lord of the 5th, is associated with 5 or more bindus and aspected by or conjoined with Jupiter. If, on the other hand, such a lord (of the house occupied by the lord of the 5th) is debilitated possessing 1 to 3 bindus, the son will prove treacherous to the father.

22. A sinful (*karmaheena*) son who will be a blot to the family will be born if the lord of the 5th is afflicted and the karaka, associated

with 1 to 3 bindus, is hemmed inbetween malefics.

Prasna Marga is more exhaustive in the treatment of Jupiter's Ashtakavarga. I shall cull out important combinations from it for the information of the reader.

It will be noticed that some of the rules given below pertaining to the determination of the number of issues are not only repetitive but also mutually contradictory. A clever and experienced astrologer should be able to reconcile apparent contradictions without much difficulty if he remembers the fact that in astrology we have to deal with a number of factors.

23. Find the number of bindus in the Rasi occupied by the lord of the 5th from Jupiter (after reduction). This represents the number of children the native will have (*cf* above where you are asked to take the total number of bindus). The conduct and nature of children will be similar to the bindu-lords.

In actual practice, this method has not been found to be quite satisfactory. Moreover, Ashtakavarga after reductions does not seem to yield as reliable results as Ashtakavarga before reduction. Hence it is better to take the figure in the 5th from Jupiter before reduction. I have given some of the methods as found in ancient books and it is left to the discretion of the intelligent readers to accept their reliability or otherwise after due tests.

24. If the 5th from Jupiter (in Jupiter's Ashtakavarga) contains more bindus, contributed by planets occupying Saturnine Rasis or Navamsas, one will have an adopted issue.

25. Total all the bindus after reductions. Subtract those found in Rasis occupied by malefics. The remainder represents the number of children.

In the Standard Horoscope, the total of the bindus is 11. Deducting the bindus in Rasis occupied by Saturn (1) and Mars (0), the remainder will be 10. The native has eight children living, one issue died and there was one abortion.

26. Take the number of bindus in the 5th from Jupiter (before reduction). Deduct the bindus donated by planets in debilitation, combustion and occupying inimical places. Increase bindus contributed by planets in exaltation, retrogression and own house. The number so arrived at denotes the number of children. The number of male and female issues will correspond to the number of bindus contributed by male and female planets.

According to *Prasna Marga*, a planet in retrogression or exaltation gives three children ;

in own house or own Navamsa or Vargottama, gives 2 children.

In the Standard Horoscope, the 5th from Jupiter has 6 bindus, the donors being Saturn, Sun, Venus, Mercury, Moon and Lagna. Saturn is in an inimical sign. Venus is in debility. Deducting 2 bindus, the remainder is 4. The Sun is Vargottama. Double the contribution of Sun (2). Mercury is Vargottama. Double his contribution (2). The total will be (8). Venus and the Moon are females. Though Mercury is a eunuch he could be considered here as representing male because he occupies a masculine sign. Hence the total number of children will be 8—6 males and 2 females.

The Ashtakavarga system no doubt provides us with a clue to the determination of the number of issues, their sexes, and the probable times of their birth. But its application can be made only to charts in which the 5th house is intrinsically strong, indicating birth of children and the horoscopes of the parents answer the best for Beeja Sphuta and Kshetra Sphuta (see *How to Judge a Horoscope* : Chapter VIII).

The 5th from Jupiter and the 5th from Lagna are the places to be looked for in judging the issues. It is the number of bindus present in these two places that signify the number of issues—the number being increased according to other benefic influences such as exaltation, own house, etc., and decreased according to malefic influences such as debilitation, combustion etc. There are horoscopes in which the 5th from Lagna and the 5th from Jupiter have a number of bindus without the natives getting any children. In such cases, the 5th house will be found to be completely afflicted. In the case of a person born[17] in 1903 the 5th from Lagna has 6 bindus (in Jupiter's Ashtakavarga) and the 5th from Jupiter has 7 bindus. The native has married four wives. But he has no issues. In this horoscope, the 5th house is occupied by debilitated Sun (lord of the 3rd) and Mercury, lord of Lagna, and aspected by Saturn, lord of the 8th. The 5th lord is debilitated in the 4th and is in association with Rahu. Putrakaraka Jupiter is in the asterism of Venus lord of the 5th who is heavily afflicted. Hence the disposition of Jupiter's Ashtakavarga has not helped matters in respect of children. But Jupiter associated with 4 bindus is fairly strong influencing favourably the 7th house matters.

In another example [19]horoscope where the general disposition of the 5th house favours the birth of issues, we find that the 5th from Jupiter has 2 bindus while the 5th from Lagna has 4 bindus. The 5th from Jupiter is occupied by the Sun lord of the 11th and the 5th lord

Saturn is debilitated. On the other hand, the 5th from Lagna is not afflicted, the 5th lord having joined the 10th with Mars lord of the 2nd and 9th. Therefore we have to consider the bindus in the 5th from Lagna. The 4 bindus have been contributed by Mars, Jupiter, Venus and Lagna, Mars, Jupiter and Lagna are not afflicted. Nor have they been glorified. Therefore the total of their contributions remains undisturbed. Venus is exalted. Therefore, his number has to be doubled. The grand total will be 5, which is correct. Jupiter is in an inimical sign and Lagna is aspected by malefic Mars. The surviving number is only 3.

A person born on [20]5-12-1914 has the 5th lord Jupiter debilitated but the house is not afflicted. Therefore, birth of children is possible. In Jupiter's Ashtakavarga, the 5th from Jupiter has 4 bindus while the 5th from Lagna has a similar number. Between the two places, the former is stronger. The 4 bindus (in the 5th from Jupiter) has been contributed by the Sun, Mars, Saturn and the Lagna. Eliminating the contributions of the Sun and Saturn, the number of issues indicated is only 2.

With reference to the horoscope[21] of a person born on 29-1-1905 we do not wish to give any explanations. The intelligent reader has to guess for himself why, despite the fact that the

5th from Lagna has 7 bindus and the 5th from Jupiter has 7 bindus, while, *prima facie* the 5th is well disposed, out of 10 issues born, only one daughter has survived.

27. There will be birth of an issue when Jupiter transits the asterism represented by the remainder obtained by dividing the product of Jupiter's Sodya Pinda and the number of bindus in the 5th from Jupiter, by 27.

In the Standard Horoscope, Jupiter's Sodya Pinda is 124. Number of bindus in the 5th from Jupiter is 6. The product of these two is (124 × 6) = 744. Dividing this by 27 and rejecting the quotient, the remainder is 15. This number counted from Aswini is Swati. When Jupiter transits this star, birth of a child is likely.

28. An issue will be born when Jupiter transits the asterism represented by the remainder obtained by dividing the product of Jupiter's Sodya Pinda by 7. If Jupiter is stronger in Navamsa than in Rasi, then count the remainder from Dhanishta and not from Aswini.

In the Standard Horoscope: 124 × 7/27 = Remainder = 4, *i.e.*, Rohini. Jupiter's transit of Rohini indicates birth of a child.

29. The month in which an issue will be born can be ascertained thus : Multiply Jupiter's Sodya Pinda by 4 and divide the product by 12.

The remainder counted from Aries represents the month.

In the Standard Horoscope: 124×4/12=496/12 : 41/4. Remainder is 4 or Cancer. When the Sun transits Cancer (17th July to 16th August) there will be birth of an issue.

30. Multiply the Sodya Pinda of Jupiter by 7. Divide the product by 27. Count the remainder from the asterism occupied by Jupiter. This will be the nakshatra in which a child is likely to be born.

In the Standard Horoscope: 124×7/27= Remainder 4. Jupiter occupies Punarvasu. The 4th from it is Makha, the likely star in which a child may be born.

31. The likely ascendant of the child will be the sign represented by the remainder obtained by dividing by 12 the product of Jupiter's Sodya Pinda and 9.

In the Standard Horoscope: 124×9/19= Remainder 12. Therefore the Lagna will be Pisces.

32. Note the lord of the* Kakshya occupied by Jupiter in the husband's horoscope and find out whether this planet has contributed a bindu

If a sign is divided into 8 equal parts, each part goes under the name of 'Kakshya' or orbit. The first and subsequent Kakshyas are ruled by Saturn, Jupiter, Mars, Sun, Venus, Mercury, Moon and Lagna respectively in the descending order.

in the 5th from Jupiter in his Ashtakavarga in the wife's horoscope. When Jupiter transits this particular sign, there will be birth of an issue.

In regard to the Standard Horoscope, Jupiter in the horoscope of the husband occupies the orbit (Kakshya) of the Sun. The Sun has contributed a bindu in the 5th from Jupiter in the Standard Horoscope. Therefore when Jupiter transits this Rasi (Libra) there will be birth of an issue.

33. The month of birth can also be ascertained thus : Note the Navamsa occupied by the lord of Kakshya (occupied by Jupiter) in the husband's horoscope. When the Sun transits the Navamsa Rasi of this Kakshya lord, or its trines, the issue will be born.

In regard to the Standard Horoscope (in the husband's chart), the Navamsa occupied by the Sun is Capricorn. Therefore the issue will be born when the Sun transits Capricorn, Taurus or Virgo.

34. Note the sign occupied by the lord of the Kakshya in which the lord of the 5th from Jupiter is placed. When Jupiter transits this sign there will be birth of an issue.

In the Standard Horoscope : Venus is in the Kakshya of Mercury who in his turn occupies

Libra. Therefore when Jupiter transits Libra, birth of an issue may happen.

35. After reductions, multiply the total bindus in Jupiter's Ashtakavarga by the figure n the 5th from Jupiter and divide the product by 12. The remainder counted from Aries represents the month in which birth of an issue s likely.

In the Standard Horoscope: Total bindus= 11. Bindus in the 5th from Jupiter is 2:

11 × 2 = 22/12 = 10 remainder: Capricorn. Therefore birth of an issue is likely in the month of Capricorn (10th January to 13th February).

Above are given rules for predicting the probable period—year, month, star, etc., of the birth of an issue. Whether this timing relates to the birth of the first issue or subsequent ones, should be ascertained on the basis of the current directional influences. When a particular Dasa (period) and a particular Bhukti (sub-period) shows the birth of children the probable time could be arrived at as per Ashtakavarga rules.

CHAPTER IX

Venus' Ashtakavarga

When asscciated with one or more bindus, Venus produces the following results :—

0 Bindu : Danger and destruction.
1 Bindu : Phlegmatic troubles.
2 Bindus : Aimless travelling.
3 Bindus : Enmity with officials and high-ups.
4 Bindus : Equal doses of happiness and sorrow.
5 Bindus : Association with friends.
6 Bindus : Association with agreeable women.
7 Bindus : Aquisition of jewellery and pearls.
8 Bindus : All kinds of happiness and pleasures.

1. One will command a number of vehicles throughout life if Venus is in a quadrant or trine associated with 8 bindus ; if with 7 bindus, he will be very rich. These results will not hold good if Venus, despite being associated with 8 or 7 bindus, is debilitated, combust or occupies the 12th.

[22]Lenin has Venus in a quadrant, associated with 8 bindus and this combination is totally present in his horoscope.

2. In *Keraleeya*, it is said that if Venus is disposed in a trine or a quadrant with 4, 5 or 6 bindus, one is likely to have as many marriages and if Venus is further aspected by Mars, he will have liaison with 4 or 5 women, instead of marriages.

It cannot perhaps be a coincidence that this combination should be present in the horoscope of the Nizam.[23] He is said to have a number of wives. Venus as lord of Lagna is in the 5th in conjunction with Ketu and associated with 6 bindus. Mars aspects Venus.

In the absence of affliction to Venus one will be blessed with a happy and comfortable married life.

In the Standard Horoscope, Venus in his own Ashtakavarga having 4 bindus is debilitated but there is neechabanga also. The native is blessed with a fairly happy married life and has the comforts of a house, conveyance and financial security also.

3. When Venus is in the ascendant or in the 10th with 5 or more bindus, the person will have more than one conveyance.

This appears to be a reliable combination, which has been found to be true in a large number of cases studied by us.

4. The disposition of Venus in Aries or Scorpio, with 5 or more bindus and aspected by benefics, favours acquisition of property, vehicles and wealth. Early marriage is likely if Venus is in a quadrant or a trine, associated with 4 or more bindus and devoid of the aspect of Mars.

In the Standard Horoscope, Venus is in a trine with 4 bindus and free from the aspect of Mars. The native married in her 13th year.

5. If however Venus, though debilitated in Rasi or Navamsa, is associated with 5 bindus and has the aspect or association of Mars, early marriage is not ruled out.

There is an apparent contradiction between the latter part of combination 4 and combination 5. According to the former, early marriage can happen if Venus is devoid of martian aspect. According to the latter, martian aspect is a pre-requisite. If the combinations are studied carefully one difference becomes evident, *viz*., that when Venus is afflicted by debilitation, martian aspect is desirable. I must confess that I have not applied these two combinations to a sufficiently large number of horoscopes to warrant an opinion of my own.

6. Though Venus may be associated with 8 bindus and occupy a trikona, the person will meet with many obstructions regarding marriage,

if the 2nd house from Lagna is occupied or aspected by malefics.

7. One will be blessed witn wealth, comforts and happiness, if the lord of the sign occupied by Venus, associated with 5 or more bindus, is disposed in a kendra or a trikona.

Venus occupies the 5th in the chart of the Duke of Windsor[6]. The lord of this sign happens to be Venus himself and he is associated with 7 bindus. The blessings of the Yoga mentioned in article 7 have been fully conferred on the Duke. In the horoscope of Prof. B S. Rao,[24] the lord of the sign occupied by Venus, *viz.*, Jupiter is in a kendra having obtained in Venus Ashtakavarga 4 bindus. He enjoyed almost all the blessings mentioned in combination 7.

8. One will have his wife and become poor if the lord of the sign Venus is in, occupies the 6th or 8th from Venus and is in the Lagna or in a trine therefrom.

Here the lord concerned should have 5 or more bindus.

9. Similarly, if Mars invested with 5 or more bindus (in Venus Ashtakavarga) is in the 7th, and the 5th and 7th lords are in mutual trines, one will abandon his wife.

10. If Mars or Saturn (associated with 5 or more bindus) is in the 7th and the lord of the 7th is either in the Navamsa of Mars or Saturn or is

aspected by either of the two, the wife's character will be questionable.

11. If Venus, associated with 4 bindus, is in a debilitated Rasi or Navamsa and Mars is also debilitated, the wife will be a scandalous woman.

According to some versions Mars, instead of being debilitated, should aspect Venus in the above situation.

12. One's wife will commit adultery if Venus associated with 1 to 3 bindus occupies a Navamsa of Saturn, and Mars is in the sign of Saturn.

13. A person will become addicted to other women if Venus, invested with 5 or more bindus, is in the Navamsa of Mars and Mars is in his own sign.

14. One will be highly libidinous if Venus, associated with 4 or more bindus, is exalted in Navamsa and is powerfully aspected by Mars:

In all these combinations, it occurs to us, that whenever the reference to disposition in the Rasi of a particular planet is mentioned, the Navamsa should also be considered and *vice versa.*

15. If Venus occupies the 6th, 7th, 8th or 12th, associated with 2 or 3 bindus, and the lord of the 7th is debilitated, the person will go after low-class women.

16. If Venus associated with 2 or 3 bindus is in the 6th or 8th in conjunction with Saturn, and aspected by Mars, the person cohabits a blind woman.

17. If one marries a wife hailing from a direction indicated by the sign holding the least number of bindus in the Ashtakavarga of Venus, misery, sorrow and illness will result.

18. Happiness, longevity, progeny and good fortune will result from a marriage if the bride is from a direction indicated by the Rasi having the highest number of bindus.

17 and 18 can also be interpreted thus : If the bride comes from a direction indicated by the sign (which is without a bindu of Venus) in the Lagnashtakavarga of the husband—marriage is a failure. If the said Rasi has more bindus in the Lagnashtakavarga of the husband, happiness and fame will result.

19. When one of the bindus in the 7th house from Venus (in his own Ashtakavarga) has been contributed by a planet who happens to own one's birth star (or its trines), the husband and wife will love each other.

In the Standard Horoscope, the birth star is Satabhisha ruled by Rahu. According to the dictum *Sanivad Rahu*, Saturn may be considered as the lord of the star. The 7th from Venus has

6 bindus, out of which one is contributed b
Saturn. Hence combination 19 holds good.

20. Multiply the Sodya Pinda of Venus b
the number of bindus in the 7th from Venus i
his own Ashtakavarga. Divide the product b
27. When Jupiter transits the asterism represer
ted by the remainder, marriage is likely.

21. Marriage is also likely when Jupite
transits a sign represented by the figure remair
ing when the product of Sodya Pinda and th
bindus in the 7th from Venus is divided by 12.

22. Or marriage may be likely in the Das
of the lord of the sign as arrived at under 21.

23. The month of marriage can be foun
thus: Multiply Sodya Pinda of Venus by th
number of bindus in 7th from Sun. Divide th
product by 12. When the Sun transits the sig
represented by the remainder, marriage is likel

In the Standard Horoscope, the Sody
Pinda of Venus is 61. The number of bindus i
the 7th from Venus (and also from the Sun) is 6
Therefore $61 \times 6 = 366$. Dividing this by 27, th
remainder is 15=Swati. When Jupiter transi
Swati or its trine constellation (Satabhisha c
Aridra) marriage may take place. Similarly th
Sun's transit of (6th sign) Virgo (14th Septembe
to 14th October) will favour marriage.

24. When the asterism as per 20 is transited by Saturn, ill-health, misfortune or even death may befall the husband or wife.

25. Multiply the Sodya Pinda of Venus by the bindus in the 7th from Jupiter (in Venus' Ashtakavarga). Divide the product by 27. When Jupiter transits the star indicated by the remainder, death of the partner may take place.

In the Standard Horoscope:

When Saturn transits Swati (*vide* combination 24) or its trinal star, the husband will suffer.

Sodya Pinda of Venus × bindus in the 7th from Jupiter. 61 × 4 = 244/27 = Remainder 1 = Aswini. Jupiter's transit of Aswini will cause trouble to husband and his death (if other factors warrant).

CHAPTER X

Saturn's Ashtakavarga

The following results happen when Saturn is associated with different numbers of bindus in his own Ashtakavarga :

0 Bindu or 1 Bindu : Loss of wealth, and destruction of all possessions.

2 Bindus : Incarceration and ill-health.

3 Bindus : Suffering due to children, wife and money.

4 Bindus : Happiness due to dependence on others.

5 Bindus : Gain of wealth and happiness.

6 Bindus : Head of a gang of robbers or undesirable elements or hunters.

7 Bindus : Acquisition of maid-servants, camels, etc.

8 Bindus : Leadership of people or becoming head of a city or town.

1. If Saturn occupies Lagna devoid of bindus (in his own Ashtakavarga), there will be either death or loss of wealth and suffering.

Some people interpret this stanza thus : When Saturn transits the sign devoid of bindus in his own Ashtakavarga, there will be loss of wealth or death. Others interpret it : When Saturn is in a Rasi devoid of bindus, there will be death or loss of wealth. [16]Stalin has no bindu in Scorpio in his Saturn's Ashtakavarga. When Saturn was transiting Scorpio (in 1902) Stalin's life was at stake, he was hiding himself in mountains and was imprisoned for 20 months.

2. If Saturn, invested with 1 to 4 bindus, is in a kendra or is exalted, one will have short life.

In [23]Swami Vivekananda's chart, Saturn is disposed in the 10th associated with 4 bindus. He did not live long.

3. When Saturn is in Lagna, associated with 5 or 6 bindus, one will meet with all sorts of worries, financial upsets, etc., from birth. If, however, Saturn associated with 5 to 8 bindus is debilitated or in an inimical sign, one will have long life.

4. If Saturn is associated with 8 bindus, the native becomes head of a Village Panchayat or a Municipal Commissioner or a Mayor ; if with 7 bindus, he will earn money by trade and allied activities.

5. If Saturn is powerfully disposed in Lagna, associated with 4 or 5 bindus one will always lead a life of sorrow, begging alms and suffering in travails.

6. When Saturn is debilitated in Navamsa and endowed with 5 or more bindus occupies Lagna or the 5th house, one suffers from laryngeal troubles and poverty.

7. One will not live long but will become fortunate if Saturn, endowed with 4 bindus but not exalted or occupying own house, is in Lagna or the 4th.

8. If Saturn endowed with 5 or more bindus is in a debilitated sign but is occupying and exalted or own Navamsa, one will live long, and possessed of wealth and happiness.

9. There will be influx of wealth through various sources, if Saturn, endowed with 1 to 3 bindus, in his own house or Navamsa, occupying a quadrant or a trine.

10. Kingship or an equal status will be the result when Saturn as lord of 9th and 10th has 1 to 3 bindus and occupies the 3rd, 6th or 11th house.

11. One would become a mendicant begging for his daily food if Saturn, as lord of Lagna or the 12th, is in his own house associated with 4 bindus and malefics are disposed in trines.

12. If Saturn as lord of Lagna or the 8th house is combust and occupies the Lagna or a trine, the person will always suffer from sorrows.

13. One will be a beggar throughout life if the lord of the 8th from Lagna or from Saturn is combust or occupies an inimical sign, devoid of benefic aspects.

14. If the 8th from Lagna or from Saturn is occupied by a benefic, and the lord of the 8th is strongly disposed, the person will be happy all through life.

A benefic planet in the 8th from Saturn confers pleasure and happiness in family life. If the 8th lord is powerful, there will be influx of wealth and respect from rulers.

15. One becomes a ruler or an equal to him if Saturn endowed with 5 or more bindus is in the ascendant, along with the Moon.

16. Poverty and affliction by windy complaints such as rheumatism will be the result if Saturn and Mars, endowed with 4 or more bindus, are in Aries and Capricorn respectively and the lord of the 8th is weakly disposed.

17. If Mars endowed with 1 bindu is debilitated, and aspected by or associated with Saturn, there will be intermingling of happiness and misery.

18. When Saturn is associated with 1 to 3 bindus, death is likely in a foreign place.

19. If Saturn associated with 2 to 3 bindus, occupies the 2nd is conjoined with or

aspected by the 2nd lord, one will frequent centres of pilgrimage.

20. A person will travel in foreign countries if Saturn, with 2 or 3 bindus, occupies the 10th or is connected with the 10th lord.

21. If Saturn happens to occupy the 2nd house and the lord of the 2nd is powerless (he must get less than 4 bindus in Saturn's Ashtakavarga), then the person will always be bent on committing sinful acts and the various Raja Yogas will become defunct.

Where a powerful lord of the 10th is disposed in a trine or a quadrant it enables one to command world fame, conveyances and political power.

22. Total the bindus in Saturn's Ashtakavarga (before reduction) from Lagna to the sign occupied by Saturn. Total also the bindus from Saturn till Lagna. These two numbers will indicate the age when the person is likely to suffer from diseases or misfortunes. The total of the above two figures also indicates the age of troubles.

If the end or beginning of a malefic Dasa coincides with the age represented by the above 3 figures, then death or great misfortunes are likely.

In the Standard Horoscope, bindus from Lagna to Saturn total 26 ; from Saturn to Lagna

16; and the sum of the two 42. When the native was aged 16, she suffered from typhoid for over 3 weeks. When she was 26, she suffered from a severe type of anaemia and lost a son aged 1. When she was 42, mentally she was unhappy and suffered from weakness.

The total of bindus in Saturn's Ashtakavarga (as per combination 22) in the horoscope of [23]Swami Vivekananda is 39. It is significant that he died in his 40th year.

23. Multiply the Sodya Pinda of Saturn by the bindus in the 8th house from Saturn (in Saturn's Ashtakavarga). Divide the product by 27. The remainder (or its trines) represents the asterism, the transit of which by Saturn will prove fatal to the native.

24. The remainder arrived at by dividing the product of Saturn's Sodya Pinda and the bindus in the sign occupied by Jupiter (in Saturn's Ashtakavarga) by 12 represents the Rasi, the transit of which by Jupiter may prove fatal to the native's life. The month of death can be known thus: Multiply the Sodya Pinda of Saturn by the bindus in the sign occupied by the Sun. Divide the product by 12. When the Sun transits the Rasi represented by the remainder, death is likely.

In the Standard Horoscope, Sodya Pinda of Saturn is 150:

(1) Number of bindus in the 8th from Saturn = 4.

(2) Number of bindus in the sign occupied by Jupiter = 4.

(3) Number of bindus in the sign occupied by Sun = 3.

Therefore (1) 150 × 4/27 = Remainder 6 = Aridra.

(2) 150 × 4/12 = Remainder 0 = 12 = Pisces.

(3) 150 × 3/12 = Remainder 6 = Virgo.

Therefore Saturn's transit of Aridra (Swati or Satabhisha), Jupiter's transit of Pisces and the Sun's transit of Virgo may prove critical provided the Dasa also indicates similar results.

25. If after reduction the sign occupied by Saturn and the 7th therefrom are devoid of bindus, one is likely to have an unnatural death in a solitary place. If, however, these 2 signs have aspects from friendly planets, friends will be near at the time of death. If these signs are aspected by inimical planets, the native will be surrounded by enemies at the time of death.

The following methods can also be employed for finding the probable time of death.

26. Multiply Sodya Pinda of Saturn by the number of bindus in the sign occupied by

;aturn. Divide the product by 7. The remain-ler represents the asterism, the transit of which)y Saturn may prove fatal.

In the Standard Horoscope, 150 (Sodya ?inda of Saturn) × 3 (number of bindus in the ign occupied by Saturn) = 450. This divided)y 7 leaves a remainder of 2. This represents 3harani. Saturn's transit of this star will be 'ery harmful.

It has been found in actual practice that in ıll the cases where certain transits are said to)rove fatal, misfortunes, mental affliction and llness and financial losses have occurred.

CHAPTER XI

Sarvashtakavarga

We have already learnt in Chapter II how to calculate Sarvashtakavarga. This Chakra or diagram has many uses. In the matter of interpreting the Sarvashtakavarga one has to use considerable skill. A verbatim application is not called for in astrological predictions. Years ago I had come across a pandit who could give a snapshot interpretation of a horoscope merely on the basis of Sarvashtakavarga, with considerable accuracy.

1. Bhavas associated with less than 25 bindus are not auspicious. Fairly good results are indicated if the number is 30. The results appropriate to the bhava will fully manifest if the number of bindus exceeds 30. Planets in exaltation, in own house, in quadrangular or trinal position, in upachaya places, etc., become ineffective if they are associated with less number of bindus. Planets occupying debilitation, or inimical place, 6th, 8th or 12th houses, associated with the lord of the sign Mandi is in, become capable of conferring favourable results provided they are associated with more bindus.

2. According to *Prasna Marga*, in the Sarvashtakavarga, the figures noted below are the minimum required. In general if they are exceeded, the concerned bhavas gain vitality. If the number falls short, the bhava will be weakened.

Lagna—25 ; 2nd house—22 ; 3rd house—29; 4th—24 ; 5th—25 ; 6th—34 ; 7th—19 ; 8th—24 ; 9th—29 ; 10th—36 ; 11th—54 ; and 12th—16.

In actual practice, it is rare to come across horoscopes which have 54 bindus in the 11th and 16 in the 12th. Such an uneven distribution is rare.

3. If the Lagna, the 9th, 10th and 11th houses have more than 30 bindus, then the person will lead a high-class life as long as he lives. If these houses have less number of bindus, one becomes poor, disease-stricken, and ill-tempered.

4. One will have recourse to begging if the ascendant, 9th, 10th and 11th houses are associated with 21 to 22 bindus and malefic planets are disposed in trinal houses.

5. If the ascendant has not less than 30 bindus and the 3rd a good number of them, one secures power or some sort of a "royal commission".

6. When there are 30 bindus each in the Lagna, the Moon sign, the 10th and the 11th, and the ascendant or the Moon is associated with or aspected by Jupiter, one becomes the head of a town, city or may even become a high-ranking minister.

7. One becomes a ruler if the 2nd, 9th, 10th and 11th houses are associated with 30 or more bindus each.

8. If the Lagna containing 30 or more bindus is associated with the lord of the 9th, 10th or 4th, one becomes a beacon to his family.

9. When the 4th house and the sign occupied by the lord of the 4th has more than 30 bindus and the former is occupied by a benefic and the latter is aspected by a benefic; or when the 4th, associated with 30 bindus, is aspected by Saturn and the 4th lord is in a quadrant, one will be blessed with all comforts of life.

10. One will suffer from sores, venereal complaints, etc., if the lord of the 8th or a quadrant is associated with 25 to 30 bindus and Mars aspects the 8th.

11. When the Moon is in the 3rd associated with 30 bindus and aspected by the Sun and Saturn, the person suffers from sores and windy complaints.

12. If the third house associated with 25 to 30 bindus is aspected by Saturn, one suffers from urinary complaints.

13. The Moon being combust and the lord of the Moon-sign, devoid of strength, is aspected by Saturn, the person suffers from evil spirits.

14. Fame, wealth and happiness will be vouchsafed when the 11th house has more bindus than the 10th, but the 12th has less number of bindus than the 11th and when the bindus in the ascendant are greater than those in the 12th.

15. Pisces to Gemini, Cancer to Libra and Scorpio to Aquarius denote the three sections of life—childhood, youth and old age. Add together the bindus in each of these sections. That section of life (childhood, youth or old age) will be happy and prosperous whose total is the greatest.

16. According to some, this division into three sections should commence from Lagna. Yet others suggest that while totalling, the bindus in the 8th and 12th must be omitted.

In the Standard Horoscope, the first, middle and last sections get 122, 105 and 110 according to (15) and 115, 114 and 108 respectively according to (16). In either case, the happy period of life would be during her childhood, while the old age will also be fairly happy.

17. The part of life corresponding to a particular section will be happy if there are

benefics occupying any of the signs. It will give rise to happiness and misery if there are benefics as well as malefics. It will be completely unhappy if malefics alone occupy a section.

Deficiency of bindus is balanced by the situation of benefics. Excess of bindus gets neutralised by the disposition of malefics. Thus if a certain section (khanda) has the least number of bindus and in addition malefics occupy the section, the part of life corresponding to the section will be more miserable.

18. Generally when the number of bindus is less, one suffers from sickness, mental worry and disappointment. According to Garga, during the section of life corresponding to the Khanda (least number) occupied by malefics in debilitation, combustion, etc., one will suffer imprisonment, loss of wealth, etc. When the Khanda is occupied by benefics in exaltation, own house, etc., during that part of life, one will have fame, acquisition of wealth and fortune. The results will be mixed if benefics are neecha, etc., and malefics are in favourable places.

19. A person gets a conveyance, royal favour, riches and sons after the expiry of the age corresponding to the number of bindus in Lagna, provided there are appropriate combinations in the horoscope.

20. The life-span of one born in Capricorn or Aquarius will correspond to the number of bindus in Lagna if the lord of the 12th is in Lagna and the lords of Lagna and the 8th are weak.

21. When there is interchange of houses between the 1st and 4th lords, and when the signs occupied by these lords have 23 bindus each, there will be acquisition of ministership and wealth.

22. There will be acquisition of personal magnetism and great fortune after the 40th year if the ascendant, the 4th and 11th houses have more than 30 bindus each.

23. If the 4th and 9th houses have 25 to 30 bindus, then the person will acquire riches either at the end of the 28th year or some time afterwards.

24. Kingship or command over a lakh of horses will be conferred when Jupiter, endowed with 40 bindus, is exalted in the 4th, the Sun is in the ascendant and Mars occupies Aries.

25. One would become a ruler if Lagna is associated with 40 bindus, Jupiter is in Sagittarius, Venus is in Pisces, Mars is exalted and Saturn is in Aquarius.

26. Aries, Taurus, Gemini and Cancer and their trinal signs represent respectively the four directions beginning from the east. Add together

the bindus in the signs representing each direction. It is in the direction corresponding to the larger total that one will get wealth and riches. If benefics are also situated in such a direction, there will be excess of good. In the quarter represented by the sign occupied by the ascendant lord, one will have livelihood; in the quarter corresponding to the sign occupied by the 2nd lord, one will gain wealth; and in the quarter or direction corresponding to the sign occupied by the 8th lord, destruction will result.

27. The strongest dik or direction obtained as above must be chosen for building houses, etc.

28. Multiply the total of bindus from the ascendant to the sign occupied by Saturn by 7, and divide the product by 27. When the asterism represented by the remainder or its trinal one is transited by the Sun and other malefics, one suffers from illness, misfortune and other afflictions.

29. The remainder arrived at according to above process also represents the year in which one suffers from illness and troubles.

30. Add together the bindus in Raṣiṣ occupied by benefics, multiply the total by 7 and divide the product by 27. When benefics pass through the asterism represented by the remainder, happiness and fortunate events may happen.

31. Total the bindus from Saturn to Lagna, Lagna to Saturn, Mars to Lagna, Lagna to Mars, Lagna to Rahu and Rahu to Lagna, severally. In each case, multiply the sum by 7 and divide the product by 27. The *quotient* in each case represents the age at which sorrow, fatigue, ill-health, misunderstandings, injuries from weapons, etc., will befall the native. Similar results take place when malefics transit the asterism represented by the remainder.

In the Standard Horoscope: (1) the total number of bindus from Lagna to Saturn will be (24+27+31+33+25+33+30+26)=229; (2) from Saturn to Lagna the total will be (26+23+26+29+30+24)=158. Multiplying (1) and (2) severally by 7 and dividing the product by 27, we get

		Remainder	Quotient
I.	(1)	10th (Makha)	59
	(2)	26th (Uttarabhadra)	40

Ill-health, misunderstandings, etc., are indicated at the age of 40 and 59 and also when Saturn, Mars and other malefics transit Makha and Uttarabhadra. Rahu and Mars similarly reckoned give the following figures :—

II. (1) Mars to Lagna = 83

$$\frac{83 \times 7}{27} = \text{Quotient } 21$$

Remainder 14

(Chitta)

(2) Lagna to Mars = 307

$$\frac{307 \times 7}{27} = \text{Quotient } 79$$

Remainder 16

(Visakha)

III. (1) Since Rahu is in the same sign as Mars, figures obtained in II hold good.

Therefore at the age of 21 and at 79 and also when malefics transit Chitta and Visakha, the evil results suggested in combination 30 are likely to materialise.

32. Add together the bindus from Saturn to the sign occupied by the lord of the 8th from Saturn. The remainder obtained by dividing the product of this sum and bindus in the 8th house from Saturn denotes the star which when transited by Sun indicates the time of death of the native.

33. Deal with benefic planets as per article 31. The age represented by the *quotient* and the periods when benefics transit the asterism denoted by the remainder indicates auspicious happenings, happiness, success, birth of issues, professional prosperity, etc.

In the Standard Horoscope, taking Jupiter, the figures will be

(1) Lagna to Jupiter 173

(2) Jupiter to Lagna 221

Therefore (1) $\frac{173 \times 7}{27}$ = Quotient 44
Remainder 23
(Dhanishta)

(2) $\frac{221 \times 7}{27}$ = Quotient 57
Remainder 8
(Pushya)

The 44th and 57th years and the times when Jupiter transits Dhanishta and Pushyami should prove prosperous, auspicious and happy.

34. Multiply the figures (after reductions—see Chart 21) in the signs occupied by the lords of the 8th, 4th and 11th by figures (before reduction) in the 8th, 4th and 11th respectively and divide the product in each case by 12. The remainder represents the month counted from Aries in which the native, his father and mother respectively may pass away.

In the Standard Horoscope, the figures in the signs occupied by the lords of the 8th (Virgo), 4th (Scorpio) and 11th (Scorpio) are (after I reduction) respectively 10, 0 and 0. Multiplying these figures by 26, 33 and 29 respectively—these are the figures in the 8th, 4th and 11th (before reduction in Sarvashtakavarga) —and dividing the products by 12, we get 8, 9 and 5 as remainders indicating Scorpio, Sagittarius and Leo as the months for the deaths of the native, his father and mother respectively.

35. Multiply the Sodya Pinda of Sarvashtakavarga by the bindus (B.R.) in a particular bhava and divide the product by 27. When Saturn transits the asterism represented by the remainder, evil results pertaining to the bhava in question will materialise.

In the Standard Horoscope, the Sodya Pinda of Sarvashtakavarga (see Chapter XIV) is 412. Let us take the Lagna. It has 24 bindus.

$\frac{412 \times 12}{27}$ leaves a remainder of 6 = Aridra.

Saturn's transit of not only Aridra but its trinal stars, Swati and Satabhisha, should adversely affect the first bhava indications.

Studies conducted by me in respect of Jupiter's transit of asterisms as arrived at above have been found to be mainly favourable for the bhavas concerned. Such transits on the basis of Ashtakavarga if combined with directional influences appear to yield encouraging results.

36. Deal as above with the Sodya Pinda in respect of *rekhas* in Sarvashtakavarga (Chart No. 22). When Saturn transits the asterism

represented by the remainder the effects of the concerned bhava will improve.

In the Standard Horoscope, the Sodya Pinda of the rekhas is 269 (*vide* Chapter XIV). Take for instance the 10th bhava. It has 30 rekhas. Multiplying this number by the Sodya Pinda and dividing the product by 27, we get

$\frac{269 \times 30}{27}$ = Remainder 24 or Satabhisha.

When Saturn transits this star or its trines, *viz.*, Aslesha or Jyeshta, the 10th house gains vitality with the result events signified by the bhava should prosper. Other bhavas can be similarly treated.

37. According as the 8th bhava is occupied by Rahu, Mars and Saturn, the native is likely to be poisoned, undergo surgical treatment or suffer miseries and ill-health at the age corresponding to the number of bindus in the sign occupied by the concerned planets.

In the Standard Horoscope, the 8th house is occupied by Saturn. It contains 26 bindus. The native was not poisoned but she suffered from a most serious type anaemia which persisted for 2 months.

38. At the age corresponding to the figures in the signs occupied by Jupiter, Venus and Mercury, the person will enjoy wealth, fame and children ; have marriage or marital happiness ; and acquire education, honour and fame.

CHAPTER XII

Timing Events

Prastharashtakavarga can be put to two improtant uses, *viz.*, for the delineation of Dasa results and for predicting Gochara or Transit effects. The timing of an event could be narrowed down to as brief an interval as possible. Opinions vary as regards the nature of events produced by the transiting planets in the light of directional indications, but I shall confine myself to an enumeration of results as I have gathered from my discussions with learned astrologers and based on my own humble studies. Much information on the interpretation of Dasa results in the light of Prastharashtakavarga is not available in classical works. Therefore what I give here is only intended to offer a certain basis upon which intelligent astrologers can further develop.

In this book unless otherwise stated, Dasa means the Vimshottari system, widely in use today and not the Ashtakavarga Dasa system. Ayurdaya revealed by Ashtakavarga has not been found to be quite reliable. Ashtakavarga Dasa is based on the terms of life granted by different planets as per Ashtakavarga system and hence it is not quite safe to relay on the Ashtakavarga Dasa. But when the reference is to a sub-period, it may connote either the sub-period of a planet as per Vimshottari or the division of a Dasa period symbolically into 8 or 12 parts as explained in the following paragraphs :—

Main Periods

1. Consider the usual astrological factors such as ownership, location, association, aspect, etc., in respect of the lord of Dasa.

2. If the sign occupied by a Dasa lord (in his own Ashtakavarga) has a large number of bindus, the results will invariably be favourable.

3. Find out the Kakshya occupied by the Dasa lord. If there is a bindu in this particular Kakshya (in the Dasa lord's Ashtakavarga), the lord will be inclined to confer favourable results.

Sub-periods

1. The sub-period of a planet associated with less than the optimum number of bindus (in the Ashtakavarga of the major lord) will generally prove inauspicious in respect of events signified by

(*a*) the bhavas owned by the sub-lord,
(*b*) the bhava the sub-lord is in, and
(*c*) the bhava whose lord has not contributed a bindu to the sign occupied by the sub-lord in the lord's Ashtakavarga.

2. The sub-period of a planet associated with more than 4 bindus will give favourable results such as reputation, financial success, health, political power, etc., and such events as are signified by

(*a*) the bhavas owned by the sub-lord,

(*b*) the bhavas occupied by the sub-lord, and

(*c*) the bhava whose lord has contributed a bindu to the sign occupied by the sub-lord, in the Dasa lord's Ashtakavarga.

The bindu strength (of the lord or the sub-lord) is capable of neutralising the blemish due to occupation of Dusthanas or places of debilitation, etc., while the deficiency of bindus may bring down the Raja Yoga and other favourable trends which the planets concerned are otherwise capable of.

It is also to be noted that if both the signs owned by a sub-lord are associated with bindus, the vitality of the sub-lord is enhanced. This rule does not of course apply to the Sun and the Moon.

As already observed above an important factor contributing to the strength or otherwise of a major lord is the donation or otherwise of a bindu by the lord of the Kakshya in which the Dasa lord is situated. If the contribution has been made, the discretion of the Dasa lord will be strengthened to give effect to the results as ɔer *a*, *b*, *c* listed above ; otherwise there will be certain obstruction.

These directional influences should always ɔe interpreted taking into account transit indiations.

In the Standard Horoscope, let us take upiter's Dasa. It lasts from 30-7-1930 to 0-7-1946. Jupiter as lord of the 3rd and 12th from Lagna) is blemished. But as lord of the nd and 11th from Chandra Lagna, he is not ad. By occupation—6th from Lagna and 5th rom Moon—he is fairly well disposed. The esults to be caused by him would pertain to he 3rd (brothers), 12th (loss and dishonour, tc.), 5th (children), 11th (gains) and 6th lisease, success over enemies, etc.). In his own shtakavarga, Jupiter has been associated with bindus and hence extremely auspicious, so that e overall results will have to be favourable. In ct in the course of Jupiter's Dasa, while she as married and begot children, entered family fe and improved financially, there were also appenings which caused her extreme anxiety, nhappiness and misunderstandings. The indiations of the 12th threatened to fully materialise ut Jupiter's inherent auspiciousness enabled the ative to tide over all the difficulties. It will be en that Jupiter is in 23° 35′ of Gemini occupying the Kakshya of the Moon and the Moon has contributed a bindu minimising Jupiter's afflictions to some extent.

Let us take the sub-period of Saturn (according to Vimshottari) in the major period of Jupiter. This lasted from 18-9-1932 to 30th May 1935. The sub-lord owns the Lagna (health body, etc.) and 2nd (finance and family) and is actually in the 7th bhava (husband). In Jupiter's Ashtakavarga, Saturn has 4 bindus. Hence both good and bad results can happen, the good pertaining to the events signified by Jupiter, Mars, Mercury and the Moon and unfavourable results pertaining to Saturn, Sun, Venus and Lagna. The native's father underwent difficulties when he entered family life. The husband passed a higher examination and the subject fell seriously ill. Both the signs owned by Saturn have bindus. Hence the sub-period as a whole proved auspicious.

Some scholars opine that the period of a Dasa can be divided into 8 equal parts in the order of the orbits of the different planets from the earth. According to this scheme, the first and subsequent parts will be symbolically ruled by Saturn, Jupiter, Mars, Sun, Venus, Mercury, Moon and the Lagna. This means the duration of each sub-period will be one-eighth of the Dasa period and irrespective of the Dasa, the first and subsequent sub-periods will be in the above order.

In the Standard Horoscope, Jupiter's Dasa period divided according to the order of Prasthara can be tabulated thus :—

Main period :—Jupiter (30–7–1930 to 30–7–1946).

Sub-divisions :—

		1930–7–30
I	Saturn	2–0–0
		1932–7–30
II	Jupiter	2–0–0
		1934–7–30
III	Mars	2–0–0
		1936–7–30
IV	Sun	2–0–0
		1938–7–30
V	Venus	2–0–0
		1940–7–30
VI	Mercury	2–0–0
		1942–7–30
VII	Moon	2–0–0
		1944–7–30
VIII	Lagna	2–0–0
		1946–7–30

In Jupiter's Ashtakavarga, Saturn has not contributed a bindu to the sign occupied by Jupiter. Hence the first two years (in the Dasa of Jupiter covered by Saturn's Kakshya) should be adverse. But Saturn's two Rasis (in Jupiter's Ashtakavarga) have 5 and 4 bindus respectively so that the evil referred to above gets neutralised. Saturn is the lord of Lagna and is in the 8th from Lagna and 7th from the Moon. Hence the nature of results likely to happen will pertain to these houses. In fact she married as soon as Jupiter's Dasa commenced. The indications of Dasas should be interpreted in the light of the transit influences also.

Another Method

According to some, the Dasa period of a planet can be divided into 12 parts covering the 12 houses and starting from the Rasi occupied by the planets concerned. The first twelfth part of the Dasa will produce results pertaining to the bhava to which the Rasi occupied by the lord has reference. Thus in the Standard Horoscope, taking Saturn's Dasa and dividing it into 21 parts, each part or sub-period extends for 19 months. Saturn is in Leo, the 8th from the ascendant. The results of the first sub-period will pertain largely to the 8th house. The nature of the results depends upon the minimum, optimum or maximum number of bindus contained in a particular Rasi (in the Ashtakavarga of the planet concerned) covered by a particular sub-period. Again taking the Standard Horoscope, we find that Leo or Simha has only 3 bindus in

Saturn's Ashtakavarga. This is less than the optimum. The native had a period of worry, sickness and disappointments. The third sub-period has reference to Libra, which happens to be the 10th house. Libra has 5 bindus which is more than the optimum. During this sub-period, honours befell the native's husband. There was acquisition of a house, birth of a daughter and generally favourable period.

Research work done in this particular method of Dasa interpretation has yielded interesting facts. In a large number of cases studied—there have been exceptions too—it has been found that while the general trend of results indicated in a particular sub-period pertains to the events signified by the bhava which has reference to the Rasi covered by the sub-period, the planets contributing *bindus* to the Rasi covered are also capable of producing results mainly of their karakatwa and to a certain extent of the bhavas they own, occupy or aspect.

In the III sub-period (30th September 1949 to 30th April 1951) referred to above covered by Libra (the 10th from Lagna) while generally favourable results were produced by virtue of Libra containing 5 bindus, the exact nature of the results corresponded to the karakatwa signification) of Mars (lands and houses),

Jupiter (issues), Sun (reputation) and Moon (mental peace). It will be seen that the 5 bindus in Libra (in Saturn's Ashtakavarga) are made up of contributions by Saturn, Jupiter, Mars, the Sun and Lagna.

It has also been found that if a sub-period is divided into 8 parts in the order of Prasthara Ashtakavarga (*see* p. 115) the planet, that has contributed a bindu, is capable of giving rise to the results of its karakatwa (or ownership and situation) in the particular interval governed by it. Thus in the Standard Horoscope, we can divide the sub-period of Saturn's Dasa thus:

Dasa (period)—Saturn
Sub-period—Libra (III)
No. of bindus in Libra—5.

Date of commencement of sub-period 30–9–1949.

I	Interval (Saturn) (in the descending order of Prasthara)	1949–9–30
		0–2–11¼
		1949–12–11¼
II	Interval (Jupiter)	0–2–11¼
		1950–2–22½
III	Interval (Mars)	0–2–11¼
		1950–5–3¾
IV	Interval (Sun)	0–2–11¼
		1950–7–15

		1950–7–15
V	Interval (Venus)	0–2–$11\frac{1}{4}$
		1950–9–$26\frac{1}{4}$
VI	Interval (Mercury)	0–2–$11\frac{1}{4}$
		1950–12–$7\frac{1}{2}$
VII	Interval (Moon)	0–2–$11\frac{1}{4}$
		1951–2–$18\frac{3}{4}$
VIII	Interval (Lagna)	0–2–$11\frac{1}{4}$
		1951–4–30

In the first interval governed by Saturn, othing untoward happened because though laced in the eighth and ruling Lagna, Saturn as contributed a bindu. In the second interval –Jupiter has contributed 1 bindu and Jupiter is ord of the 2nd and 11th and occupies the 5th rom Chandra Lagna and aspected by Mars uling over lands and properties—there was cquisition of a house and also birth of an issue. t can also be anticipated that during the interals of planets who have not contributed a indu either adverse or ordinary results can appen. The health of the native suffered in he 6th interval (Mercury). It will be seen that Iercury has not donated a bindu.

It occurs to me that this method of interreting Dasas offers a vast field for research ork. In considering the results to happen ither in the entire period as a whole, or in a sub-period covering a Rasi, or in an interva spread over $\frac{1}{8}$th of a sub-period, due attentio must be paid to the transits also. In a subjec like astrology, where events happening in th lives of human beings have to be read, no fas and hard rules can be laid down. With th astrological dicta as propounded in classica works as our guide-posts, we have to desig methods capable of timing events with as muc accuracy as possible.

CHAPTER XIII

Transits or Gochara

Innumerable methods of interpreting results of transits or Gochara have been enumerated in classical astrological texts. It is not my intention either to decry or glorify them. In a subject like astrology, the dependability of methods must rest upon the accuracy of results obtained. Delineation of results by considering the movements of planets from Janma Rasi or the radical Moon has invariably been a rule rather than an exception with the rank and file of astrologers in India. The factor of *latta* or the dominant nature of the directional influences is hardly considered. It is not for me to comment on the reliability or otherwise of such methods of transit interpretations.

By transit is meant the passage or movement of planets. They take varying periods for moving from one sign to the other. Such movements may give rise to certain changes in the generation and distribution of forces which in their turn are bound to produce their own effects on mankind in general and individuals in particular. It must be noted that Gochara or transit results, however, powerful, are always subordinate to the radical or birth influences. Some astrological texts claim that irrespective of directional influences, planets while in transit can produce results, good, bad or indifferent, according to the particular places transited by them, both with reference to the Moon and with reference to the situation of the different planets at the time of birth. Such a view cannot be tenable in the light of facts and experience. I think, the approach of *Prasna Marga* to the subject of Gochara in the light of Ashtakavarga is fairly systematic and scientific.

There are two factors to be considered in interpreting Gochara effects, *viz.*, (*a*) the Ashtakavarga of the planet concerned and (*b*) the malefic or benefic nature of the place transited.

The following are the results likely to be produced by the Sun and other planets when they transit different signs from the sign occupied by the Moon at the time of birth.—

The Sun.—(1) Financial loss, discomfort, chest pain and aimless journey; (2) increase of expenditure, eye trouble, deceit and unhappiness; (3) increase of emoluments, freedom from sickness and destruction of enemies; (4) quarrels with wife, unhappiness in conjugal life and the general ailments; (5) increase of enemies and physical indisposition; (6) success over enemies, joy and good health ; (7) wearisome travelling, chest pain and stomach troubles ; (8) misunderstandings with or separation from wife ; (9) accidents, stomach trouble, mental worry and opposition ; (10) success in endeavours, honour and realisation of ambition ; (11) great success, respect, freedom from disease and prosperity ; and (12) success by right means, have means of character.

The Moon.—(1) Good food, comforts and clothes ; (2) loss of respect, money and increase of obstacles ; (3) domestic happiness and access to money ; (4) loss of trust in others and lack of peace of mind ; (5) indisposition, grief and disappointment; (6) happiness, success over enemies and good health ; (7) respect from others and sudden influx of unexpected resoures ; (8) apprehension, uneasiness and worry ; (9) mental pain, stomach trouble and incarceration (if there is an indication in the horoscope) ; (10) success, authority and position, realisation of ambition ; (11) prosperity, new friends and good income ; and (12) injuries due to fall from vehicles and increased expenditure.

Mars.—(1) Troubles from various sources and bodily affliction ; (2) trouble from the Government, frequent quarrels with enemies, disease, accidents, bilious and windy complaints and loss by theft; (3) benefits through auspicious characters, financial improvement and acquisition of woollen articles and also authority ; (4) fever, stomachache, piles and blood discharges and frequent trouble from ailments; (5) trouble from enemies, illness, misunderstandings with children and loss of physical energy ; (6) success over enemies, termination of strife in the family, and acquisition of self-confidence ; (7) frequent quarrels with wife, eye trouble and stomachache; (8) loss of blood from piles and anaemia and loss of wealth and name ; (9) suffering from insults, heavy expenditure and weakness due to ill-health; (10) acquisition of money from unexpected source ; (11) fame, reputation and authority ; and (12) unforeseen expenses, quarrels with wife, eye disease and bilious affections.

Mercury.—(1) Loss of money due to advice by wicked men, worry due to association with tale-bearers, quarrels, imprisonment and disagreeble news while travelling ; (2) disgrace, ill-treatment from relatives but acquisition of success and wealth ; (3) new friends, but anticipation of trouble from government and enemies, aimless roaming about due to misdeeds ; (4) prosperity for relatives and family members, addition to family and gain of money ; (5) quarrels with wife and children ; (6) gain of renown, success and popularity; (7) bloodlessness, quarrels and mental uneasiness ; (8) birth of an issue, success, happiness and acquisition of new articles ; (9) obstacles and mental worry ; (10) defeat of enemies, acquisition of money, happiness with wife and agreeable company ; (11) acquisition of wealth; birth of a son and happiness ; and (12) disgrace from enemies, disease and domestic disharmony.

Jupiter.—(1) Loss of money and intelligence; aimless roaming about and frequent quarrels ; (2) happiness, domestic harmony and success over enemies ; (3) moving about from place to place, obstacles to own work and loss of position ; (4) troubles from relatives, development of a sense of resignation to the inevitable ; (5) acquisition of servants, birth of a son, general prosperity, addition of property and development of good qualities ; (6) affliction of mind, friends turning enemies and indifferent to good things ; (7) happiness, erotic pleasure, good income, purchase of a conveyance and graceful speech ; (8) imprisonment, disease, heavy grief and serious illness ; (9) influential, birth of an issue, success in work and acquisition of wealth from an unexpected source ; (10) destruction of position, loss of money and health and aimless roaming about ; (11) reinstatement in former position, and recovery of health ; and (12) fall from ideals and right conduct and increase of grief.

Venus.—(1) Acquisition of comforts for pleasure, and a happy life ; (2) acquisition of money and gifts, birth of an issue, and erotic pleasure ; (3) influence, wealth and respect ; (4) disgrace to enemies and general prosperity ; (5) renewal of contact with friends, increase of reputation, influence and power ; (6) general happiness, extension of business, birth of an issue and good income ; (7) humiliation, disease and danger; (8) injuries and trouble from women and mental worry ; (9) acquisition of a new house, articles of luxury and wife if not married ; (10) increase of virtue, happiness, wealth and performance of religious acts ; (11) quarrels and disgrace; (12) acquisition of new friends, money, perfumes and clothes.

Saturn.—(1) Fear from poison or fire, of friends and family members, fear of incarceration, travel to foreign lands, loss of money and near relatives; separation from kith and kin and suffering from insults ; (2) emaciated physical appearance, loss of comfort, acquisition but not enjoyment of wealth; (3) increase of wealth and other comforts, good health, general happiness and disappearance of enemies ; (4) separation from friends and family members, suspicious nature, crooked behaviour and wicked acts ; (5) separation from sons, loss of money and frequent quarrels; (6) freedom from enemies and diseases, association with fair sex; (7) separation from wife and children and aimless roaming about; (8) indulgence in mean activities and bereft of happiness; (9) same results as in (8), suffers from hatred, heart trouble and even imprisonment; (10) gets new avocation, but loses money and fame; (11) frequent loss of temper but acquisition of wealth through wrong means; and (12) grief, series of miseries, ill-health and general affliction.

The above results are general and they should be carefully applied to individual horoscopes in the light of directional influences and Ashtakavarga dispositions. When there are no combinations for incarceration in the birth of horoscope, imprisonment indicated by a transit should not be predicted. Similarly when there are no powerful yogas in the radical chart, reputation, fame, etc., denoted by a transit will have a very limited scope for expression.

When a planet transits a Rasi, declared favourable and has less than 4 bindus in his own Ashtakavarga, the favourable results will be minimum. If the number is 4, they will be optimum and if more than 4 the maximum. Similarly if a planet transits an unfavourable place, but has bindus in it, the malefic effects are proportionately reduced, depending upon the number of bindus in it. Conversely, a favourable transit in a Ṛasi devoid of bindus reduces the benefic effects while an unfavourable transit in such a Rasi will further increase the malefic effects.

For example, in the Standard Horoscope, the Sun's transit of Aries (3rd from Moon) should prove favourable. In the Sun's own Ashtakavarga, there are 5 bindus in Aries. Therefore the good effects produced should be to the extent of 62%. The Sun's transit of Capricorn (12th from the Moon) should prove adverse. Capricorn has no bindus. Therefore the evil results to be produced by this transit are to the brim.

This is only a general method of gauging the extent of benefic or malefic results a transiting planet is capable of.

According to classical texts, the following results are supposed to be produced when planets transit Rasis with different bindus.

In Sun's Ashtakavarga, when the Sun transits a Rasi having 8 bindus, the effects will be wealth and prosperity and royal favour ; 7—welfare, happiness and pomp ; 6—rising power ; 5—wealth; 4—both good and bad will be equal ; 3—fatigue through journey ; 2—sinful actions ; 1—severe sickness, and no bindu—death.

Similarly in Moon's Ashtakavarga when Moon transits a Rasi with 8 bindus—happiness, prosperity and help from relatives ; 7—gain of clothes, agreeable food and gain of perfumes; 6—study of Mantras and association with religious heads; 5—courage and mental satisfaction; 4—misery and ill-health; 3—quarrels with relations; 2—quarrels brought about by one's wife and one's wealth; 1—irreparable losses; and no bindu—sorrow and extreme panic.

When Mars transits a Rasi with 8 bindus—gain of landed property and moneys, acquisition of a house and victory; 7—prosperity through brothers; 6—favour through kings; 5—pleasing experiences; 4—good and bad in equal proportion; 3—separation from brothers and women; 2—quarrels due to wife and wealth; 1—disease; as smallpox, etc.; and no bindu—disease in the stomach, fits and exhaustion.

When Mercury transits a Rasi with 8 bindus—respect from rulers; 7—increase of wealth and learning; 6—success attending all efforts; 5—reconciliation with relations; 4—want of spirit in everything; 3—anxiety through disturbed thoughts; 2—diseases caused by mental worry; 1—imprisonment by force and unexpected calamities; and no bindu—unexpected loss of everything and consequent mental worries.

When Jupiter transits a Rasi with 8 bindus—sovereignty, ownership and kingly prosperity; 7—gain of wealth and happiness; 6—gain of clothes, vehicles and gold ; 5—ruin to enemies, accomplishment of desired objects ; 4—gain and loss in equal measure ; 3—nervous debility and ear diseases ; 2—royal frowns ; 1—loss of wealth and relations ; and no bindu—derangement of the mind, loss of wealth and children.

When Venus transits a Rasi with 8 bindus—comfort from good clothes, women, flowers and wholesome food ; 7—gain of ornaments and pearls ; 6—happiness from agreeable wife ; 5—meeting with friends ; 4—equal dose of good and bad ; 3—quarrel with the people of the locality and relatives ; 2—diseases and dismissal from service ; 1—fear from water and poison ; and no bindu—all sorts of calamities.

When Saturn transits a Rasi with 8 bindus—acquisition of administrative control over a village or town ; 7—acquisition of servants and domestic animals ; 6—popularity with "thieves, hill tribes and army chief" ; 5—gain of grain ; 4—good and bad equal ; 3—loss of wealth, servants, women and happiness ; 2—imprisonment, fear and disease ; 1—dirty fallen life ; and with no bindu—ill-luck in everything.

As per the above description Mars transiting a Rasi with 3 bindus denotes "separation from brothers and women." Suppose the Rasi happens to be the 12th from the Moon and directional influences also do not indicate such evil result or the native has no brothers and sisters. In such cases, the astrologer must have recourse to commonsense and modify judgment.

Usually, when a planet transits a sign, which has the highest number of bindus in its Ashtakavarga, it advances results of the bhava represented by the Rasi as reckoned from the ascendant.

In the Standard Horoscope, the ascendant is Capricorn and the Moon is in Aquarius. In Jupiter's Ashtakavarga, there are 6 bindus in Cancer. Suppose Jupiter transits Cancer. This happens to be the 6th from the Moon indicating "affliction of the mind and friends becoming enemies". But the sign happens to be the 7th from Lagna. Hence misunderstandings with the husband and mental uneasiness on that account may be expected. But there are six bindus. This neutralises the evil to the extent of 75% and therefore evil results are reduced to the minimum while "gain of gold vehicles" could also be anticipated.

We have already seen that according to the scheme of Prasthara Chakra, each sign of the zodiac stands divided into 8 parts or Kakshyas (of $3\frac{3}{4}°$ each) in the order of Saturn, Jupiter, Sun, Venus, Mercury, Moon and the Lagna. In its each transit of a sign, a planet has to pass through each Kakshya in the above order. The number of bindus in a Rasi (in regard to the Ashtakavarga of any planet) is the sum-total of the contribution of each planet and the Prasthara Chakra reveals the planets that make the contribution.

In the Standard Horoscope, there are 4 bindus (in Jupiter's Ashtakavarga) in Aquarius and the Prasthara Chakra of Jupiter makes it clear that these 4 bindus have been distributed by Mars, Venus, Mercury and Lagna. Jupiter entered Aquarius on 19-2-1962 and his transit of different Kakshyas in this sign will be thus approximately :

Kakshya	*Longitude*	*Period of Transit*
1. Saturn	300° 0′ to 303° 45′	19-2-1962 to 4-4-1962
2. Jupiter	303° 45′ to 307° 30′	4-4-1962 to 19-6-1962
3. Mars	307° 30′ to 311° 15′	19-6-1962 to 4-8-1962
4. Sun	311° 15′ to 315° 0′	4-8-1962 to 19-9-1962
5. Venus	315° 0′ to 318° 45′	19-9-1962 to 4-11-1962
6. Mercury	318° 45′ to 322° 30′	4-11-1962 to 19-12-1962
7. Moon	322° 30′ to 326° 15′	19-12-1962 to 4-2-1963
8. Lagna	326° 15′ to 330° 0′	4-2-1963 to 17-4-1963

Jupiter's transit of Janma Rasi is generally not favourable. It indicates "loss of money, mental balance and position, and frequent quarrels". Here the sign happens to be the Lagna and the effects must largely pertain to the first bhava. But there are 4 bindus in Aquarius so that the evil is offset to the extent of 50%, gain and loss being in equal measure. When Jupiter transits the Kakshya of Saturn (19-2-1962 to 4-4-1962) there will be sickness (because Saturn has not contributed a bindu), pain in the body and financial loss (because Saturn owns the 12th). When Jupiter transits the 2nd Kakshya—his own—(4-4-1962 to 19-6-1962) unfavourable results can be expected because Jupiter is not only lord of the 3rd and 12th but has contributed no bindu. Good income can be predicted when Jupiter transits the 3rd Kakshya ruled by Mars (19-6-1962 to 4-8-1962). There will be gain of land and worry on account of children. Mars has also contributed a bindu and hence, the evils get largely minimised.

There is a school of thought according to which the results also partake of the karaka characteristics of the planet contributing a bindu. I think there is much truth in this view. It has also been found that a planet contributing a bindu produces the result of the bhava it aspects much more than the bhava it occupies. Thus in the Standard Horoscope, during Jupiter's ransit of the Kakshya of himself (because he spects the 2nd in the birth chart) the native had ome financial losses. During the period of upiter's transit of Saturn's Kakshya, because of aturn's aspect on the 5th house, the native had lot of anxiety in regard to children.

The following results culled out from classical texts will be found to be useful in reading ochara :—

1. When Saturn transits a Rasi which has no bindus (in Mercury's Ashtakavarga after reduction) there will be serious illness to brothers, children and friends.

2. A planet transiting a sign can give beneficial results only during the period of its passage through the Kakshyas, the lords of which have contributed bindus.

3. When four or more planets simultaneously transit Kakshyas (in their own respective Ashtakavargas) whose lords have contributed bindus, increasing good results happen.

4. When a planet transits a sign having bindus in his own Ashtakavarga he is capable of producing effects :

(*a*) due to karakatwa ;

(*b*) due to house disposition with reference to the sign occupied by the Kakshya lord ; and

(*c*) due to location from Lagna at the time of transit.

For example, let us take the Sun's transit in the Standard Horoscope. He is in Virgo. Suppose he transits Gemini (14th June to 15th July). In each Kakshya he remains for 3 days and 18 hours. Gemini has 5 bindus contributed by Saturn, Mars, Sun himself, Mercury and Lagna. Therefore the transit effects will be :

(*a*) due to the karakatwa of Sun (*vide* p. 33)

(*b*) in the first $3\frac{3}{4}$ days, he transits Saturn's

Kakshya. Saturn who has contributed a bindu is in Leo. The Sun's transit has reference to the 11th from Saturn and hence favourable. When he transits the Kakshya of Mars—Mars has also contributed a bindu and the Sun is in the 11th from Mars—favourable results are likely ; and (c) the Sun's transit has reference to the 6th from Lagna, so that 6th house indications can come to the fore.

5. The beneficial effects of transits get accentuated if the sign transited, in addition to containing bindus, also happens to be the place of planet's own house or exaltation ; the effects will be correspondingly low if the sign happens to be the place of debilitation.

6. Where the Kakshya lord and the transiting planet are friends, the results will be highly beneficial. Otherwise, the effects will be adverse.

In the Standard Horoscope, when the Sun transits the Kakshya of Saturn though Saturn has contributed a bindu, the Sun happens to be an enemy of Saturn and hence there will be a certain toning down of the good effects.

7. Generally Mercury's transits of a Kakshya devoid of a bindu gives rise to quarrels and nervous debility.

8. Sickness to brothers and other evil results happen at the time of Saturn's transit of a sign devoid of bindus (after reductions in

Mercury's Ashtakavarga).If the said sign happens to be the 8th or 12th from the Moon, the person suffers from ill-health.

9. Jupiter's transit of a Kakshya without a bindu (in his own Ashtakavarga) gives rise to mental worry, financial distress, increase of expenditure and trouble through careless talk.

10. Inheritance of a legacy can take place at the time of Saturn's transit of a Kakshya containing a bindu (in his own Ashtakavarga). If the Kakshya has no bindu, there will be accidents, fall from elevations, injuries from weapons, quarrels and misunderstandings.

11. Note the sign containing the least number of bindus in Saturn's Ashtakavarga. Everyday when that Rasi is at the horizon, the native will suffer from some mental annoyance or other.

12. The intensity of evil results produced during the period 7½ years' Saturn gets minimised if the 12th, 1st and 2nd from the Moon has more than 30 bindus in the Sarvashtakavarga.

The transits of Jupiter and Saturn are of primary importance while those of the other planets will have a secondary importance. It is the combined effects of the transits as well as the directions, that can indicate, for any given period, the nature of the results to happen. The reader will do well to work out a number of horoscopes, taking into account past events so that he could himself test how far the method of timing events, expounded in this book, actually hold good.

CHAPTER XIV

Longevity Determination

There are several species of Ayurdaya recommended by ancient astrological writers, such as Ashtakavargayu, Jeevasarmayu, Piṇḍayu, Naisargikayu, Amsayu, etc. In classical works on astrology as many as 32 methods have been mentioned. Ancient authorities are not agreed as to which of these various methods are fool-proof and universally applicable. In our humble view, mathematical methods of longevity determination cannot be relied upon safely. While Amsayu has yielded correct results in a number of cases, longevity determined according to Ashtakavarga has not been found satisfactory in many cases.

A number of methods have been given in classical works for calculating Ayurdaya according to Ashtakavarga. I do not propose to deal with them all as they are not only cumbersome but in my view, superfluous.

In the course of this chapter, I shall confine myself to two methods, one based on Bhinnashtakavarga (Method *A*) and the other based on the Sarvashtakavarga (Method *B*). It is for the intelligent reader to find out for himself how far each method can be relied upon for accuracy.

Method A

The essentials to be considered are Rasi Gunakara (zodiacal factors) and Graha Gunakara (planetary factors).

We have to consider for the purpose of ascertaining these factors, the Bhinna or individual Ashtakavargas of planets after reduction.

Rasi Gunakara

Each sign of the zodiac has a number assigned to it as its Rasi Gunakara or zodiacal factor as given below :—

Aries	7	Cancer		Libra	7	Capricorn	5
Taurus	10	Leo	10	Scorpio	8	Aquarius	11
Gemini	8	Virgo	5	Sagittarius	9	Pisces	12

These numbers are constant for all horoscopes.

The bindus left (after the two reductions) in the several signs from Aries, in the Ashtakavarga of each planet, must be multiplied by the respective zodiacal factor and all the 12 products must be added together

In the Standard Horoscope, the Sun's Ashtakavarga stands thus after I and II reductions (*vide* p. 18).

0	0	3	2
2	Sun's Ashtakavarga after I and II Reductions		0
0			0
0	1	0	4 Sun

Applying the above rules to the Sun :—

Sign (Rasi)	*No. of bindus*	×	*Zodiacal Factor (Rasi Gunakara)*	=	*Zodiacal Product (Rasi Pinda)*
Aries	0	×	7	=	0
Taurus	3	×	10	=	30
Gemini	2	×	8	=	16
Cancer	0	×	4	=	0
Leo	0	×	10	=	0
Virgo	4	×	5	=	20
Libra	0	×	7	=	0
Scorpio	1	×	8	=	8
Sagittarius	0	×	9	=	0
Capricorn	0	×	5	=	0
Aquarius	2	×	11	=	22
Pisces	0	×	12	=	0
			Total zodiacal product		96

Applying the same rules to the other planets, we get their zodiacal products as follows :

Moon 80, Mars 126, Mercury 97, Jupiter 79, Venus 66 and Saturn 170.

Graha Gunakara

Just as each Rasi has a multiplier (Rasi Gunakara or zodiacal factor) so also each planet has also been assigned a multiplier (Graha Gunakara or planetary factor). Multiply the several figures in the signs occupied by the various planets (after I and II reductions) by the figures of the planetary factors. Add the seven products together.

The planetary factors (Graha Gunakara) are :—

Sun	5	Mercury	5		
Moon	5	Jupiter	10	Saturn	5.
Mars	8	Venus	7		

In the Standard Horoscope, the Sun is in Virgo ; the Moon in Aquarius ; Mars in Scorpio; Mercury in Libra ; Jupiter in Gemini ; Venus in Virgo ; and Saturn in Leo. Taking the Ashtakavarga table of the Sun (after reductions) there are 4 bindus in Virgo, the sign occupied by the Sun. Multiplying this by the Sun's planetary factor, *viz.*, 5, we get 5×4=20. The Moon is in Aquarius which has 2 bindus. Therefore multiplying this by 5, the planetary factor of the Moon, we get 5×2=10. Applying the same rules to the other planets, we get :—

Planet (Graha)	Sign (Rasi)	Bindus (benefic points)		Planetary Factor (Graha Gunakara)		Planetary Product (Graha Pinda)
Sun	Virgo	4	×	5	=	20
Moon	Aquarius	2	×	5	=	10
Mars	Scorpio	1	×	8	=	8
Mercury	Libra	0	×	5	=	0
Jupiter	Gemini	2	×	10	=	20
Venus	Virgo	4	×	7	=	28
Saturn	Leo	0	×	5	=	0
					Total	86

The total planetary product (Graha Pinda) of all these will be 86. This is in respect of the Sun's Ashtakavarga. From the Ashtakavargas of other planets, we get their Graha Pindas as Moon 20, Mars 71, Mercury 61, Jupiter 45, Venus 0, and Saturn 42.

The sum of the Rasi figures (Rasi Pinda) and Planetary figures (Graha Pinda) will be the Sodya Pinda for each planet.

* Multiply the Sodya Pinda of a planet by 7 and divide the product by 27. The quotient represents the gross years of longevity contributed

* According to *Jataka Parijata*, the Sodya Pinda of a planet must be divided by 30 and the quotient represents Ayus (longevity) given by the planet concerned. If the quotient exceeds 12, divide it by 12 and take the remainder: (*a*) Double the number, if the planet is exalted. (*b*) Halve it if the planet is debilitated, combust or eclipsed. (*c*) Calculate proportionate period if between exaltation and debilitation.

by the planet concerned. If the quotient exceeds *27, it must be reduced by 27.

Taking the Sun in the Standard Horoscope:

Rasi figure	....	96
Graha figure	....	86
Sodya Pinda	....	182

182 × 7/27 = years 47.20.

This number exceeds 27. Therefore deduct 27 from it. We get the Sun's term of longevity as 20.20 years. In the Standard Horoscope, the gross terms contributed by the planets are :—

The Sun		20.20 years
The Moon	....	26.00 years
Mars	....	24.00 years
Mercury	....	14.00 years
Jupiter	....	5.00 years
Venus	....	15.80 years
Saturn	....	12.00 years
Total	....	117.00 years

Haranas or Reductions

The number of years obtained above are subject to certain haranas or reductions due to the aspects, conjunctions, etc., the planets are involved in :

* According to *Sambhu Hora*, if the quotient exceeds 27 (but less than 54), subtract it from 54; if it is more than 54 (but less than 81) subtract it from 81 and if the quotient is more than 81 (but less than 108) subtract it from 108. In actual practice, this system has not been found to be quite satisfactory.

(*a*) If there is more than one planet in a sign, its term of life should be reduced by one half.

(*b*) If a planet is debilitated or in combustion, one half must be deducted.

(*c*) If a planet is in the sign of an enemy, its term of life must be reduced by one-third.

(*d*) If a malefic planet is in the visible half of the zodiac reduce its Ayurdaya years thus :—12th house—full ; 11th—one half ; 10th—one-third ; 9th—one-fourth ; 8th—one-fifth ; and seventh—one-sixth. A benefic in the visible part of the zodiac loses half of what a malefic does.

(*e*) If a planet suffers defeat in Graha Yuddha (planetary war), one-third must be deducted.

(*f*) If the Sun or the Moon is of unusual appearance (as in eclipse) one-third of the term of life must be deducted.

When the same planet is subject to several reductions, the highest reduction should be applied.

In the Standard Horoscope, the Sun is subject to (*a*), Mars and Mercury to (*d*), Venus to (*a*), (*b*) and (*d*) and Saturn to (*c*). As Venus is subject to three reductions, the highest alone (*a*) should be carried out.

Applying these reductions to the Standard Horoscope :—

Planet	Gross years	Nature of reduction	How much	Net years
The Sun	20.20	(*a*)	1/2	10.10
The Moon	26.00	—	—	26.00
Mars	24.00	(*d*)	1/2	12.00
Mercury	14.00	(*d*)	1/6	11.67
Jupiter	5.00	—	—	5.00
Venus	15.80	(*a*), (*b*), (*d*)	1/2	7.90
Saturn	12.00	(*c*)	1/3	8.00
			Total	80.67

Multiply the net years got above by 324 and divide the product by 365, to convert Chandramana (lunar measure) years to Sauramana (solar measure). In the Standard Horoscope the longevity of the native will be

$$\frac{80.67 \times 324}{365} = 71.6 \text{ years}$$

Method B

The other method of determining longevity, according to Ashtakavarga, is known as Naksharayus. Find as usual Sodya Pinda of the Sarvashtakavarga Chart No. 21 (after carrying out the I and II reductions). Multiply the net figures by planetary and zodiacal factors. Total the products. Multiply this aggregate by 7 and divide the product by 27. Diminish the quotient (if it exceeds 100) by 100. Multiply the resulting figure by 324 and divide the product by 365. This will give Nakshatrayus of the person.

In the Standard Horoscope, the net figures of Sarvashtakavarga are treated as follows for obtaining the Sodya Pinda (Chart No. 21) of the Sarvashtakavarga.

Planetary Factors
(Chart No. 21)

Planet	*Sign*	*Bindus*	×	*Planetary Factor*		*Planetary Product*
Sun	Virgo	10	×	5	=	50
Moon	Aquarius	1	×	5	=	5
Mars	Scorpio	0	×	8	=	0
Mercury	Libra	0	×	5	=	0
Jupiter	Gemini	7	×	10	=	70
Venus	Virgo	10	×	7	=	70
Saturn	Leo	0	×	5	=	0
		Total of Graha Pinda			....	195

Zodiacal Factors (Chart No. 21)

Sign	*No. of (A.R.) Bindus*	×	*Zodiacal Factor*	=	*Zodiac Produ*
Aries	7	×	7	=	49
Taurus	0	×	10	=	0
Gemini	7	×	8	=	56
Cancer	1	×	4	=	4
Leo	0	×	10	=	0
Virgo	10	×	5	=	50
Libra	0	×	7	=	0
Scorpio	0	×	8	=	0
Sagittarius	2	×	9	=	18

Sign	No. of (A.R.) Bindus	×	Zodiacal Factor	=	Zodiacal Product
Capricorn	1	×	5	=	5
Aquarius	1	×	11	=	11
Pisces	2	×	12	=	24
			Total	...	217

Graha Pinda + Rasi Pinda = Sodya Pinda

195 + 217 = 412

Sodya Pinda of Sarvashtakavarga = 412.

Multiplying 412 by 7 and dividing the product by 27, we get—

$$\frac{412 \times 7}{27} = 106.80 \text{ years.}$$

Again multiplying this by 324 and dividing the product by 365, we get—

$$\frac{106.80 \times 324}{365} = 94.8 \text{ years.}$$

This is the Nakshatrayu of the native.

Rekha Sodya Pinda

Just as the Sodya Pinda of bindus (in Sarvashtakavarga) is found so also the Sodya Pinda of Rekhas (in Sarvashtakavarga) can also be determined from the chart of Rekhas (*vide* page 21, Chart 22). The use of the Sodya Pinda of Rekhas has been explained on page 108.

In the Standard Horoscope the net figures of Rekhas (*vide* pages 21 & 22) are treated as follows for obtaining the Sodya Pinda of Sarvashtakavarga Rekhas.

Rasi Pinda of Rekhas

	Rekhas		Zodiacal Factor
Aries	2 × 7	=	14
Taurus	0 × 10	=	0
Gemini	6 × 8	=	48
Cancer	1 × 4	=	4
Leo	4 × 10	=	40
Virgo	2 × 5	=	10
Libra	1 × 7	=	7
Scorpio	2 × 8	=	16
Sagittarius	0 × 9	=	0
Capricorn	1 × 5	=	5
Aquarius	0 × 11	=	0
Pisces	0 × 12	=	0
Rasi Pinda (zodiacal product) ..			144

Graha Pinda of Rekhas

	Rekhas		Planetary Factor
Sun	2 × 5	=	10
Moon	0 × 5	=	0
Mars	2 × 8	=	16
Mercury	1 × 5	=	5
Jupiter	6 × 10	=	60
Venus	2 × 7	=	14
Saturn	4 × 5	=	20
			125
	Rasi Pinda....		144
	Graha Pinda....		125
	Sodya Pinda of Rekhas....		269

It must be noted that the Ashtakavarga system of Ayurdaya generally does not hold good in actual practice. The methods are described with an example for the understanding of the student of astrology. Research work alone can reveal the defects of this system. Correct assessment of longevity should be based upon the various Yogas and directional influences as per Vimshottari. Mathematical methods alone are no right royal road.

CHAPTER XV

Miscellaneous

The Sun

1. When the Sun transits signs having 5, 6, 7 or 8 bindus, the period will be auspicious to undertake long journeys, to conduct marriages and to initiate other good actions.

2. When the Sun transits signs having 3, 2 or 1 bindu, actions done will generally not end well. If there is no bindu, the period is absolutely forbidden for undertaking work of any auspicious nature. If the number is 4, the outcome will be both good and bad.

3. Installation of the Deity of Siva in the direction signified by the Rasi holding the largest number of bindus favours progress in spiritual matters.

4. Total the number of bindus (*a*) in the four consecutive signs beginning from the sign occupied by the Sun; (*b*) in the next four signs from the 5th, (*c*) and the next four signs from the 9th. If the first total is greater than the 2nd or the 3rd, the first part of the day will be good for doing any auspicious work, such as performance of marriage, interviewing important

persons, etc. If the 2nd is greater than the 1st or 3rd, the second part of the day will be good. And if the 3rd is greater, the 3rd part of the day is good. The part of the day corresponding to the least total should be rejected for any good work.

The Moon

5. When the Moon transits signs having 6, 7 or 8 bindus, the time will be propitious for celebrating one's marriage, to employ assistants, to begin studies and to make friendships.

6. The above actions done when the Moon passes through Rasis with 1, 2 or 3 bindus will prove fruitless.

7. Interviews done in the early morning with persons born in Rasis which in the native's horoscope are associated with more bindus (in the Moon's Ashtakavarga) will prove fruitful or beneficial.

8. If the bridegroom's Janma Rasi happens to be the one which, in the bride's horoscope, is associated with maximum bindus, the married life will be happy. Similar results ensue if the bride's Janma Rasi happens to be one which, in the horoscope of the bridegroom, has a large number of bindus (in Moon's Ashtakavarga).

Mars

9. The period covered by the martian transit of a Rasi (in his own Ashtakavarga) con-

taining the highest number of bindus will be favourable for buying lands, houses and other immovable properties and for embarking on litigation.

10. It will also be beneficial if the kitchen is located in that direction represented by the sign having the highest number of bindus.

Mercury

11. Education, literary work, debates, etc., commenced when Mercury transits a Rasi associated with largest number of bindus will be successful. This period will also favour success in litigation. The month in which the Sun passes through the said Rasi will also be favourable.

12. For getting the grace of Lord Vishnu, He should be propitiated at the time when the sign containing the maximum number of bindus in Mercury's Ashtakavarga is rising.

Jupiter

13. When Jupiter passes through a sign which has the maximum number of bindus in his Ashtakavarga, the period will be highly propitious for getting spiritual initiation, for making penance, for initiating studies in Vedas, for earning money, for performance of religious ceremonies and for begetting children.

14. The direction indicated by the sign having the largest number of bindus in Jupiter's

Ashtakavarga would be suitable for keeping jewels and money.

15. Everyday, the time at which the sign referred to in article 13 will be auspicious for doing prayer, worship, recitation of Japa, etc. This particular time favours success in all these matters.

16. Sexual intercourse, done during the time mentioned in 15, will result in the birth of a child.

Venus

17. When Venus transits a sign in his Ashtakavarga, associated with the largest number of bindus, learning of music, celebration of marriage and purchase of clothes, bedding, etc., must be done.

18. The direction suggested by the sign referred to in 17 will be favourable for having one's bedroom in one's house, for getting a bride, and for meeting distinguished personages.

Saturn

19. It is advisable to acquire factories, and begin agricultural operations when Saturn transits a Rasi having the maximum number of bindus in his Ashtakavarga.

20. In one's residence, the quarter, represented by the sign mentioned in 19, will be suitable for constructing water-closets, latrines

and for keeping agricultural implements and storing fuel.

Sarvashtakavarga

21. Treatment begun when the Rasi containing the least number of bindus in the Sarvashtakavarga is rising, results in early recovery.

22. For good actions, journeys and for all auspicious functions, select the time when the Rasis having more than 30 bindus in Sarvashtakavarga are rising.

Rahu's Ashtakavarga

There is no mention of Rahu's Ashtakavarga in most of the standard works on astrology. But *Sambhu Hora Prakasa* takes into account Rahu also in its treatment of the Ashtakavarga. Standard authorities have agreed that the total number of bindus is 337, given by the seven planets with reference to themselves and the Lagna. As Rahu is only a *Chaya Graha* (or a node), the exclusion of Rahu from the scheme of Ashtakavarga is understandable. I shall deal with Rahu also for the information of the readers, though it does not form part of the general Ashtakavarga scheme.

In Rahu's Ashtakavarga, his benefic places from the Sun are 1st, 2nd, 3rd, 5th, 7th, 8th and 10th; 1st, 3rd, 5th, 7th, 8th, 9th and 10th from the Moon ; 2nd, 3rd, 5th, 7th and 12th from Mars ; 2nd, 4th, 7th, 8th and 12th from Mercury ; 1st 3rd, 4th, 6th and 8th from Jupiter ; 6th, 7th, 11th and 12th from Venus ; 3rd, 5th, 7th, 10th, 11th and 12th from Saturn ; and 3rd, 4th, 5th, 9th and 12th from Lagna.—Total 44 points.

It will be seen from the above that while the auspicious places have been reckoned from the seven planets and Lagna, there is no reckoning from Rahu himself. The reductions and reduced figures are considered in respect of the seven planets and not Rahu. Hence there is no need to carry out the Trikona and Ekadhipatya Sodhana in regard to Rahu's Ashtakavarga.

In the Standard Horoscope, Rahu's Ashtakavarga stands thus :—

4	4	4	4
3	Chart No. 26		2
4 Lagna			3
3	4 Rahu	4	5

The above bindus can be used for estimating the results of Rahu's period by the application of the methods suggested in Chapter XI.

A Prasthara Chakra of Rahu can also be prepared but no Kakshya has been assigned to him. Rahu's transit in the Kakshyas of the seven planets and the Lagna could be considered for interpreting Gochara results as given in Chapter XII. While transiting the 12 places from Janma Rasi or radical Moon, Rahu is said to give rise to the following results :—

(1) Sickness and fear, (2) loss of wealth, quarrelling and misunderstandings, (3) happiness and good tidings, (4) sickness, danger and sorrow, (5) financial loss and worry, (6) pleasure and happiness, (7) loss and fear, (8) danger to life, (9) quarrelling, mental worry and loss, (10) enmity, (11) happiness and acquisition of money, and (12) expenses and danger.

When Rahu transits a sign, because of his backward motion, he passes through each of the Kakshyas for about 2¼ months in the order of Lagna, Moon, Mercury, Venus, Sun, Mars, Jupiter and Saturn unlike the planets which have regular movements. The results to be given rise to depend upon the position of the sign transited with reference to the Moon and the bhava which this sign happens to be from Lagna. Passage

IN THE STANDARD HOROSCOPE THE FOLLOWING IS THE PRASTHARA CHAKRA

	Scorpio Rahu Mars	Sagittarius	Capricorn	Aquarius Moon	Pisces	Aries	Taurus Ketu	Gemini Jupiter	Cancer	Leo Saturn	Virgo Venus Sun	Libra Mercury	Total
Saturn		0		0			0	0	0			0	6
Jupiter	0		0					0		0	0		5
Mars		0	0		0		0					0	5
Sun	0		0		0	0		0			0	0	7
Venus				0	0					0	0		4
Mercury	0		0			0	0		0				5
Moon	0			0		0		0		0	0	0	7
Lagna		0			0	0	0				0		5
Total	4	3	4	3	4	4	4	4	2	3	5	4	44

through a Kakshya devoid of a bindu gives rise to evil results while the contrary will be the case when transiting a Kakshya containing a bindu.

For example, let us consider Rahu's transit of Cancer in the Standard Horoscope. Rahu entered Cancer on 1-1-1961. His passage through the different Kakshyas will be as follows :—

Kakshya	*Longitude*	*From*	*To*
Lagna	30° to 26° 15′	1-12-1961	5-2-1962
Moon	26° 15′ to 22° 30′	5-2-1962	17-4-1962
Mercury	22° 30′ to 18° 45′	17-4-1962	27-6-1962
Venus	18° 45′ to 15° 00′	27-6-1962	6-9-1962
Sun	15° 00′ to 11° 15′	6-9-1962	16-11-1962
Mars	11° 15′ to 7° 30′	16-11-1962	25-1-1963
Jupiter	7° 30′ to 3° 45′	25-1-1963	6-4-1963
Saturn	3° 45′ to 0° 0′	6-4-1963	16-6-1963

Rahu's transit of the 6th from the Moon is generally favourable. It indicates "pleasure and happiness". This transit has reference to the 7th house. Therefore the benefic results will pertain to the 7th house. There will be harmony in domestic life and the native will have happy relations with her husband. When Rahu transits a Kakshya which has no bindu, there will be a lessening of these beneficial results.

Rahu transited the Kakshya of Lagna from 1-12-1961 to 5-2-1962. Lagna has not contributed a bindu. Therefore the "pleasure and happiness" due to transit in the 6th from the Moon is reduced. Lord of Lagna Saturn has only three bindus in Rahu's Ashtakavarga. Rahu is aspecting the fifth—house of children—in the radical chart. Therefore during this period, there will be an intermingling of benefic and malefic results bearing on health, children and the husband. Whether or not to consider Rahu's Ashtakavarga is left to the discretion of the intelligent reader.

Illustrated Horoscopes

No. 1. An Eminent Indian

Birth Details—Born on 8/9–12–1878 at 5–40 a.m. (L.M.T.) (Lat. 12° 45′ N., Long. 78° 54′ E.).

Planetary Positions :—*The Sun 237° 8′; the Moon 59° 24′; Mars 209° 24′ ; Mercury 257° 54′ ; Jupiter 285° 11′ ; Venus 238° 11′ ; Saturn 335° 31′ ; Rahu 285° 45′; and Ascendant 229° 16′. Ayanamsa 20° 42′. Balance of Mars' Dasa : 3 years, 9 months, 23 days.

Ashtakavarga Figures—**The Sun*: 5, 5(2), 4, 3(1), 4(2), 5(2), 6(2), 5(3), 2, 3, 4, 2. *The Moon*: 4(1), 4, 3, 6(3), 6(3), 4, 3, 3, 5(1), 4, 4(1). *Mars*: 5(2), 2, 3, 2, 3(1), 4, 6(5), 4(2), 2, 4(2), 1, 3(1). *Mercury*: 5, 2, 6(2), 3, 5, 5(2), 5(1), 6(3), 6(1), 3(1), 4, 4(1). *Jupiter* : 5(1), 5, 2, 6(1), 7(3), 5, 3(1), 5, 4, 5, 4(2), 5. *Venus*: 2, 4. 6, 4, 5(3), 6, 4, 4, 5(3), 4, 4, 4. *Saturn* : 2, 4(2), 2, 4(2), 5(3), 5(3), 3(1), 4(2), 3(1), 2, 3(1), 2. *Sarvashtakavarga*: 28(4), 26(4), 26(2), 28(7), 35(15), 34(7), 30(10), 31(10), 25(5), 26(4), 24(3), 24(3).

SODYA PINDAS

	Sun	Moon	Mars	Mercury	Jupiter	Venus	Saturn
Rasi Pindas :	92	66	97	83	70	57	116
Graha Pindas :	62	15	89	64	8	15	47
Sodya Pindas :	154	81	186	147	78	72	163

---

* The figures against each planet indicate the bindus (before reduction) in its Ashtakavarga, counted in the order of Aries, Taurus, etc., while the figures in brackets are the bindus after the two reductions. For example, in the Illustrated Horoscope No. 1, the figures 5, 5(2), etc., against the Sun represent that in the Sun's Ashtakavarga the bindus are as follows: Aries 5, Taurus 5 (and 2 after reduction), Gemini 4, Cancer 3 (and 1 after reduction), Leo 4 (and 2 after reduction), Virgo 5 (and 2 after reduction), Libra 6 (and 2 after reduction), Scorpio 5 (and 3 after reduction), Sagittarius 2, Capricorn 3, Aquarius 4 and Pisces 2. These

No. 2. Franklin Delano Roosevelt

Birth Details—Born on 30–8–1882 at 8 p.m. (L.M.T.) (Lat. 40° 43′ N., Long. 73° 59′ W.).

Planetary Positions :—The Sun 290° 20′; the Moon 75° 5′; Mars 66° 15′ : Mercury 306° 23′ ; Jupiter 26° 10′ ; Venus 285° 16′ ; Saturn 15° 20′; Rahu 224° 55′; and Ascendant 143° 32′; Ayanamsa 20° 46′. Balance of Rahu Dasa : 6 years, 7 months, 19 days.

Ashtakavarga Figures—The Sun : 5(2), 2, 4, 6(4), 3, 3(1), 4, 5(2), 5(2), 5(3), 4, 2. *The Moon* : 5(3), 3, 5(1), 5(3), 3, 5, 6, 2, 2, 4, 5(1). *Mars* : 4(1), 2, 5(3), 3, 3, 2, 3(1), 4, 4(1), 4(2), 2, 3. *Mercury* :5(3), 4, 4(2), 4, 2, 6, 2, 7, 4(1), 6(2), 5(3), 5(1). *Jupiter* : 5(2), 4, 6(1), 5(1), 3, 5, 5, 5, 4(1), 4, 6(1), 4. *Venus*: 5, 3, 4, 3(1), 7(2), 3, 5(1), 6(4), 5, 4(1), 5(1), 2. *Saturn*: 3(1), 2, 3, 2, 6(4), 3(1), 4(1), 6(1), 2, 3(1), 3, 2. *Sarvashtakavarga* : 32(12), 20(0), 31(7), 27(6), 29(9), 25(2), 28(3), 39(7), 26(5), 28(9), 29(5), 23(2).

SODYA PINDAS

	Sun	*Moon*	*Mars*	*Mercury*	*Jupiter*	*Venus*	*Saturn*
Rasi Pindas :	84	71	57	101	46	79	72
Graha Pindas :	66	58	78	110	48	17	27
Sodya Pindas :	150	129	135	211	94	96	99

---

figures can be diagrammatically represented thus for the sake of easy reference :

2	5	5	4
4	SUN'S A.V. before Reduction		3
3			4
2	5	6	5

0	0	2	0
0	SUN'S A.V. after Reduction		1
0			2
0	3	2	2

The figures given in respect of the Ashtakavargas of all the other planets in all the illustrated charts are reckoned similarly.

No. 3. Karl Marx

Birth Details—Born on 5-5-1818 at 2 a.m. (L.M.T.) (Lat. 49° 44′ N., Long. 6° 38′ E.).

Planetary Positions—The Sun 24° 18′ ; The Moon 24° 8′ ; Mars 90° 58′ ; Mercury 40° 12′ ; Jupiter 263° 5′ (R) ; Venus 39° 2′ Saturn 325° 59′ ; Rahu 18° 39′ ; and Ascendant 302° 56′. Ayanamsa 19° 52′. Balance of Venus' Dasa : 3 years, 9 months, 18 days.

Ashtakavarga Figures—The Sun : 6(3), 5(2), 1, 4(1), 3, 3, 5(2), 3, 5, 5(4), 3. *The Moon* : 4(1), 2, 4(1), 5(1), 3, 6(1), 3, 6(1), 5(2), 4(1), 4. *Mars* : 3, 3(1), 2, 3(1), 3, 5(3), 5(1), 3(1), 3, 2, 5(3), *Mercury* : 2, 7(3), 1, (2), 4(2), 6(2), 4. 4, 4(2), 4, 6(5), 6. *Jupiter* : 5(2), 6, 5(3), 4(1), 3, 7, 2, 4(1), 6(1), 7(1), 4(1). *Venus* : 4(1), 5(3) 5(1), 4, 3, 6(1), 4, 4, 5(2), 2, 4, 6. *Saturn* : 7(7), 4(2), 3, 3(1), 0, 2, 4, 4(4), 2, 4(1), 2. *Sarvashtakavarga* : 29(12), 31(13), 22(2), 30(9) 20(3), 31(7), 33(3), 27(2), 28(11), 24(1), 35(15), 27(1),

SODYA PINDAS

	Sun	Moon	Mars	Mercury	Jupiter	Venus	Saturn
Rasi Pindas	: 103	61	77	141	79	68	120
Graha Pindas	: 82	43	35	97	63	66	147
Sodya Pindas	: 185	104	112	238	142	134	267

No. 4. Havelock Ellis

Birth Details—Born on 2-2-1859 at 8-30 a.m. (L.M.T.) (Lat. 22′ N., Long. 0° 6′ W).

Planetary Positions—The Sun 292° 34′ ; the Moon 285° Mars 340° 34′ ; Mercury 270° 34′; Jupiter 51° 4′ ; Venus 247° 3 Saturn 108° 4′ ; Rahu 310° 4′ ; and Ascendant 307° 4′. Ayanar 20° 26′. Balance of Moon's Dasa : 6 years, 2 months, 12 days.

Ashtakavarga Figures—The Sun : 4(2), 4, 4(2), 3, 2, 4, 6(4), 6 3(1), 5(1), 2, 5(2). *The Moon* : 5(1), 4(2), 3(1), 5, 5(1), 2, 4, 7(1) 3(1), 2, 5. *Mars* : 4(2), 4(3), 4(1), 3, 0, 1, 5, 5(2), 2(2), 2(1), 3 6 *Mercury* : 5, 4, 4, 3, 3, 4, 6(2), 5, 6(3), 2, 4, 4, 6(3). *Jupiter* : 4, 5 5, 4, 4, 6(2), 5, 6(2), 4, 4, 5, 4. *Venus* : 4, 5(1), 2, 2, 4, 6(2), 3, 5 5(1), 4, 6(4), 6(4). *Saturn* : 3, 4(2), 2, 3(1), 3, 3(1), 4, 6(4), 4(1 3(1), 2. *Sarvashtakavarga* : 29(5), 30(9), 24(4), 23(1), 21(1), 26 33(6), 40(14), 28(8), 24(3), 25(5), 34(12).

SODYA PINDAS

	Sun	Moon	Mars	Mercury	Jupiter	Venus	Saturn
Rasi Pindas :	112	58	127	77	36	145	81
Graha Pindas :	38	35	83	45	10	49	32
Sodya Pindas :	150	93	210	122	46	194	113

No. 5. Henry Ford

Birth Details—Born on 30-7-1863 at 2 p.m. (L.M.T.) (Lat. 42° 5′ N., Long. 83° 5′ W.).

Planetary Positions—The Sun 106° 34′ ; the Moon 209° 12′ ; Mars 127° 35′ ; Mercury 102° 32′ ; Jupiter 179° 56′ ; Venus 151° 44′; Saturn 160° 32′ ; Rahu 223° 5′ ; and Ascendant 211° 52′. Ayanamsa 20° 30′. Balance of Moon's Dasa : 2 years, 5 months, 6 days.

Ashtakavarga Figures—The Sun : 5(3), 5(2), 4, 3, 4(2), 4(1), 4, 3, 2, 3, 5(1), 6(3). *The Moon*: 5(1), 4, 4, 5(2), 2, 5(1), 3, 4(1), 4(2), 7(3): 3, 3. *Mars*: 4(1), 4(3), 4, 3, 4(1), 5(4), 0, 5(1), 3, 1, 3(3), 3. *Mercury*: 7(2), 5(4), 6, 4, 4, 5(4), 3, 6(2), 5(1), 1, 4(1), 4. *Jupiter* : 4, 6(1), 3, 6(1), 5(2), 5(2), 4(1), 6, 3, 3, 6(3), 5. *Venus* : 5(2), 6(2), 6(4), 5(2), 1, 4, 2, 5(2), 6(5), 6(2), 3, 3. *Saturn* : 3, 3(2), 3(1), 5(3), 4(2), 1, 2, 3, 2, 5(4), 6, 2. *Sarvashtakavarga* : 33(9), 33(14), 30(5), 31(8), 24(7), 29(12), 18(1), 32(6), 25(8), 26(9), 30(8), 26(2).

SODYA PINDAS

	Sun	Moon	Mars	Mercury	Jupiter	Venus	Saturn
Rasi Pindas :	113	61	108	110	84	145	80
Graha Pindas :	38	57	96	88	70	30	66
Sodya Pindas :	151	118	204	198	154	175	146

No. 6. Edward—Duke of Windsor

Birth Details—Born on 23-1-1894 at 10 p.m. (L.M.T.) (Lat. 51° 30′ N., Long. 0° 5′ W.).

Planetary Positions—The Sun 71° 24′ ; the Moon 313° 0′; Mars 339° 27′ ; Mercury 96° 40′ ; Jupiter 57° 27′ ; Venus 32° 4′ ; Saturn 177° 29′ ; Rahu 344° 57′ ; and Ascendant 283° 4′. Ayanamsa 20° 56′. Balance of Rahu Dasa : 9 years, 5 months, 12 days.

Ashtakavarga Figures—The Sun : 7(2), 2, 5(4), 3, 0, 5(3), 5(4), 5(2), 6(3), 3(1), 6(3). *The Moon* : 5(1), 3(1), 1, 5(1), 5(1), 2, 2, 8(1), 4, 5, 5(4), 4. *Mars* : 6(1), 2, 3(2), 2, 1, 3(1), 5(4), 3(1), 5, 2, 1, 6(4).

Mercury : 6(1),5(2),5(3),4, 2, 5(2), 5(2), 5(1), 6(2), 3, 2, 6(2). *Jupiter*: 4, 3, 6(1), 4, 5(1), 4(1), 5, 4, 5. 5(2), 5, 6(2). *Venu* : 4, 7(2), 3(2), 3, 3, 5, 1, 4(1), 5(1), 7, 5(4), 5(1). *Saturn*: 6(5), 2, 3, 4(2), 1, 2, 3, 2, 4, 4(2), 2, 5(3). *Sarvashtakavarga* : 38(10), 24(5), 25(12), 25(3), 17(2), 26(7), 26(10), 31(6), 35(6), 29(5), 22(8), 33(15).

SODYA PINDAS

	Sun	Moon	Mars	Mercury	Jupiter	Venus	Saturn
Rasi Pindas :	173	83	112	125	57	109	89
Grana Pindas :	59	42	47	75	26	72	34
Sodya Pindas :	232	125	159	200	83	181	123

No. 7. Sri Sankaracharya of Govardhan Mutt

Birth Details—Born on 19–3–1868 at 6–33 a.m. (L.M.T.) (Lat. 17° 43′ N., Long. 73° 20′ E.).

Planetary Positians—The Sun 338° 11′ ; the Moon 280° 3′ ; Mars 320° 41′; Mercury(R) 319° 45′; Jupiter 331° 51′; Venus 18° 17′; Saturn 225° 7′ ; Rahu 133° 22′ ; and Ascendant 345° 56′. Ayanamsa 20° 34′. Balance of Moon's Dasa : 9 years, 11 months, 17 days.

Ashtakavarga Figures—The Sun : 2, 3, 5(1), 3, 4(2), 4(1), 5(2), 6(2), 5(1), 4(1), 3, 4(1). *The Moon* : 3, 3, 5(1), 3, 4(1), 4(1), 5(2), 3, 6(1), 6(3), 3, 4(1). *Mars* : 1, 4(1), 3(3), 3, 5(4), 3, 0, 4(1), 5(1), 3, 4(4), 4(1). *Mercury*: 4, 3(1), 5, 4(2), 7(3), 2, 5, 6(4),5(1),4(2), 7(2),2. *Venus* : 5(2), *Jupiter* : 4(1), 6(1), 4, 3, 3, 6(1), 4, 5(2), 6, 5, 4, 6(3). *Venus* : 5(2), 3, 5(1), 6(3), 3, 2, 5, 4(1), 5(2), 7(5), 4, 3. *Saturn*: 3(1), 1, 4(2), 3, 2, 4(2), 2, 3, 4, 6(5), 2, 5(2). *Sarvashtakavarga* : 22(4), 23(3), 31(8), 25(5), 28(10), 25(5), 26(4), 31(11), 36(6), 35(16), 27(6), 28(8).

SODYA PINDAS

	Sun	Moon	Mars	Mercury	Jupiter	Venus	Saturn
Rasi Pindas :	97	73	147	121	74	85	82
Graha Pindas :	35	30	72	56	62	44	62
Sodya Pindas :	132	103	219	177	136	129	144

No. 8. H. H. Krishnaraja Wodiyar

Birth Details—Born on 4-6-1884 at 10-18 a.m. (L.M.T.) (Lat. 12° 0′ N., Long. 76° 38′ E.).

Planetary Positions—The Sun 53° 9′ ; the Moon 182° 56′ ; Mars

128° 54′ ; Mercury 32° 44′ ; Jupiter 101° 28′ ; Venus 92° 54′ ; Saturn 52° 52′ ; Rahu 179° 37′ ; and Ascendant 117° 40′. Ayanamsa 20° 47′. Balance of Mars' Dasa : 1 year, 11 months, 16 days.

Ashtakavarga Figures—The Sun: 3, 5(2), 5(3), 2, 4(1), 3, 2, 4(2), 6(3), 4(1), 4(1), 6(3). *The Moon* : 5(3), 5(2), 2, 5(2), 2, 5(2), 6(4), 3, 5(2), 3, 3(1), 5(2). *Mars* : 2, 5(4), 3(1), 3(1), 3(1), 4(1), 2, 2, 5, 1, 4(2), 5. *Mercury* : 4(1), 7(3), 3, 4, 5(2), 4, 4(1), 4, 3, 4, 6(3), 6(2). *Jupiter* : 5(1), 6(2), 4, 4, 7(4), 4, 4, 5(1), 3, 4, 5(1), 5(1). *Venus* : 4, 4, 2, 5(1), 4, 5(1), 5(3), 4, 4, 4, 5(3), 6(2). *Saturn* : 2, 5(3), 4(2), 3(1), 2, 2, 4(2), 2, 7(2), 2, 2, 4(2). *Sarvashtakavarga* : 25(5), 37(16), 23(6), 26(5), 27(8), 27(4), 27(10), 24(3), 23(7), 22(1), 29(11), 37(12).

SODYA PINDAS

	Sun	Moon	Mars	Mercury	Jupiter	Venus	Saturn
Rasi Pindas :	149	140	89	121	98	87	106
Graha Pindas :	38	84	85	66	62	32	72
Sodya Pindas :	187	224	174	187	160	119	178

No. 9. Pandit Jawaharlal Nehru

Birth Details—Born on 14-11-1889 at 11-20-27 p.m. (L.M.T.) (Lat. 25° 27′ N., Long. 81° 51′ E).

Planetary Positions- The Sun 211° 45′ ; the Moon 109° 30′ ; Mars 161° 27′ ; Mercury 198° 40′ ; Jupiter 256° 39′ ; Venus 188° 50′. Saturn 132° 17′ ; Rahu 74° 12′ ; and Ascendant 118° 15′. Ayanamsa 20° 51′. Balance of Mercury's Dasa : 13 years, 4 months, 20 days.

Ashtakavarga Figures—The Sun : 6(2), 6(6), 5, 3(1), 4 7(7), 3, 2, 5(1), 0, 3, 4(1). *The Moon* : 5(1), 5, 5(2), 5(4), 3, 4, 4(1), 2(1), 6(3), 6(2), 3, 1. *Mars* : 4, 5(4), 2, 2, 4, 6(5), 2, 2, 4, 1, 2, 5(3). *Mercury* : 5, 6(3), 4, 5(2), 5, 4(3), 7(3), 3, 5, 1, 5(1), 4(1). *Jupiter* : 2, 3, 5(1), 7(2), 5(3), 3, 5(1), 5, 5(3), 6(3), 4, 6. *Venus* . 2, 5(1), 5, 5(1), 6(4), 4(2), 6(1), 5(1), 3(1), 2, 5, 4. *Saturn* : 2, 5(1), 4, 3(1), 4(2), 5(3), 3(1), 3(1), 4(2), 2, 2, 2. *Sarvashtakavarga* : 26(3), 35(15), 30(3), 30(11), 31(9), 33(20), 30(7), 22(3), 32(10), 18(5), 24(1), 26(5).

SODYA PINDAS

	Sun	Moon	Mars	Mercury	Jupiter	Venus	Saturn
Rasi Pindas :	134	91	101	97	95	88	82
Graha Pindas :	71	67	40	70	67	68	76
Sodya Pindas :	205	158	141	167	162	156	158

No. 10. Benito Mussolini

Birth Details—Born on 29-7-1883 at 2 p.m. (L.M.T.) (Lat. 41° 0′ N., Long. 16° 0′ E.).

Planetary Positions—The Sun 105° 13′ ; the Moon 48° 21′; Mars 52° 13′ ; Mercury 104° 43′ ; Jupiter 87° 43′ ; Venus 90° 43′ ; Saturn 46° 43′ ; Rahu 196° 4′ ; and Ascendant 21 ° 43′. Ayanamsa 20° 47′. Balance of Moon's Dasa : 3 years, 8 months, 26 days.

Ashtakavarga Figures—The Sun : 4, 4(2), 4, 2, 4, 2, 4, 4(2), 4, 5(2), 6(2), 5(3). *The Moon*: 5(4), 5, 2, 4(1), 1, 7(2), 5(3), 3, 2(1), 6(1), 4(1), 5(1). *Mars*: 3, 6(4), 2(1), 1, 3, 3, 1, 6(5), 5(2), 2, 3(2), 4(2). *Mercur* 3, 6(3), 6(4), 2, 5(2), 3, 2, 7(5), 6(3), 3, 5(3), 6(3). *Jupiter*: 6(1), 5(, 3, 5, 6(1), 5(2), 3, 5, 5, 3, 3, 7(2). *Venus*: 4(1), 4, 3, 5(2), 3, 6(2), , 3, 4(1), 5(1), 5(1), 7(1). *Saturn* : 5(3), 4(2), 2, 4(2), 2, 3(1), 5(2), 2, 2, 4(2), 4(2). *Sarvashtakavarga*: 30(9), 34(13), 22(5), 23(5), 24(3), 29(7), 23(5), 30(12), 28(7), 26(4), 30(11), 38(14).

SODYA PINDAS

	Sun	Moon	Mars	Mercury	Jupiter	Venus	Saturn
Rasi Pindas :	104	100	152	218	71	62	114
Graha Pindas :	36	17	82	94	36	34	70
Sodya Pindas :	140	117	234	312	107	96	184

No. 11. M. S. Golwalkar

Birth Details—Born on 18/19-2-1906 at 4-34 a.m. (L.M.T.) (Lat 21° 8′ N., Long. 79° 5′ E.).

Planetary Positions—The Sun 308° 15′ ; The Moon 254° 30′ ; Mars 349° 21′ ; Mercury 306° 37′ ; Jupiter 36° 42′ ; Venus 309° 22′ ; Saturn 313° 37′ ; Rahu 119° 17′; and Ascendant 274° 57′. Ayanamsa 21° 6′. Balance of Venus' Dasa : 18 years, 3 months, 0 days.

Ashtakavarga Figures—The Sun : 3, 3, 3, 2, 3, 5(2), 7(4), 5(3), 5(2), 4(1), 3, 5(3). *The Moon*: 6(1), 5(4), 5, 3(1), 5, 3, 3, 6(1), 7(2), 1, 3, 2. *Mars*: 4(3), 2, 4, 3, 1, 3, 5(2), 3, 5(4), 3(1), 3, 3. *Mercury*: 5(1), 3, 5, 3, 2, 4, 8(4), 4(1), 6(4), 5(2), 4, 5(2). *Jupiter*: 5(2), 4(1), 7(3), 5, 3, 3, 6(1), 5, 5(2), 4(1), 4, 5. *Venus*: 5, 4, 3, 3, 3, 5(1), 4(1), 5, 6(3), 5, 5(2), 4(1). *Saturn* : 3(1), 3, 2, 4(1), 2, 3, 4(2), 3, 5(3), 4, 3( ), 3. *Sarvashtakavarga* : 31(8), 24(5), 29(3), 23(2), 19, 26(3), 37(14), 31(5), 39(20), 26(5), 25(3), 27(6).

SODYA PINDAS

	Sun	Moon	Mars	Mercury	Jupiter	Venus	Saturn
Rasi Pindas :	121	77	76	113	78	63	63
Graha Pindas :	34	50	20	36	20	67	37
Sodya Pindas :	155	127	96	149	98	130	100

No. 12. Sri Narasimha Bharathi

Birth Details—Born on 11-3-1858 at 9 p.m. (L.M.T.) (Lat. 13° 0′ N., Long. 77° 35′ E.).

Planetary Positions—The Sun 330° 23′ ; the Moon 283° 45′ ; Mars 216° 55′ ; Mercury 317° 53′ ; Jupiter 22° 58′ ; Venus 333° 7′ ; Saturn 91° 6′(R); Rahu 327° 21′; and Ascendant 192° 50′. Ayanamsa 2′ ° 26′. Balance of Moon's Dasa : 7 years, 2 months, 7 days.

Ashtakavarga Figures—The Sun: 3, 2, 4, 4, 5(2), 5(3), 4, 4, 5(2), (2), 4, 4. *The Moon* : 3, 4, 3, 5(1), 4(1), 5, 3(1), 5(1), 6(3), 5(1), 2, 4. *Mars*: 2, 3(1), 3, 4(2), 4(2), 2, 3, 2, 4, 4(2), 4(1), 4(2). *Mercury* 4(2), 4(1), 4, 6(2), 5(3), 2, 5(1), 7(3), 2, 5(3), 6(2), 4. *Jupiter* : 4(1), 5(1), 6(2), 5(2), 3, 4, 4, 8(5), 5(2), 4, 5(1), 3. *Venus* : 5(2), 4(1), 3, 3, 3, 3, 6(1), 5(2), 5(1), 6(3), 5(2), 4(1). *Saturn* : 2, 1, 2, 2, 4(2), 5(4), 4(2), 3(1), 4, 5(4), 2, 5(3). *Sarvashtakavarga* : 23(5), 23(4), 25(2), 29(7), 28(10), 26(7), 29(5), 34(12), 31(8), 33(15), 28(6), 28(6).

SODYA PINDAS

	Sun	Moon	Mars	Mercury	Jupiter	Venus	Saturn
Rasi Pindas :	63	61	83	130	110	105	118
Graha Pindas :	10	18	49	79	65	73	64
Sodya Pindas :	73	79	132	209	175	178	182

No. 13. Sri Ramana Maharshi

Birth Details—Born on 29/30-12-1879 at 1 a.m. (L.M.T.) (Lat 9° 50′ N., Long. 78° 51′ E.).

Planetary Positions—The Sun 257° 4′ ; the Moon 89° 58′ ; Mars 23° 16′ ; Mercury 234° 36′; Jupiter 317° 57′; Venus 211° 57′; Saturn 348° 32′; Rahu 265° 23′; and Ascendant 182° 18′. Ayanamsa 20° 43′ Balance of Jupiter's Dasa : 4 years, 1 month, 20 days

Ashtakavarga Figures—The Sun: 5(1), 2, 3(2), 5(2), 4, 4, 6(5), 3 5(1), 5(3), 1, 5(2). *The Moon*: 1, 6(1), 4(3), 4(1), 7(6), 5, 1, 3, 4(3), 5, 5(4), 4(1). *Mars* : 5(3), 2, 2, 3, 2, 4(2), 5(3), 4(1), 3(1), 4(2), 2, 3.

Mercury: 5(2), 3, 2, 6(1), 3, 5(2), 5(3), 7(2), 4(1), 7(4), 2, 5. *Jupiter*: 6(1), 3, 2, 7(3), 6(1), 4(1), 4(2), 4, 5, 3, 7(5), 5(1). *Venus*: 2, 3, 6(2), 5(2), 4(2), 5, 5(1), 5(2), 5(3), 5(2), 4, 3. *Saturn*: 3, 1, 4(3), 5(4), 5(2), 4, 4(3), 1, 3, 5(4), 1, 3(2). *Sarvashtakavarga*: 27(7), 20(1), 23(10), 35(13), 31(11), 31(5), 30(17), 27(5), 29(9), 34(15), 22(9), 28(6).

SODYA PINDAS

	Sun	*Moon*	*Mars*	*Mercury*	*Jupiter*	*Venus*	*Saturn*
Rasi Pindas :	114	181	79	94	115	104	125
Graha Pindas :	33	75	41	45	63	49	25
Sodya Pindas :	147	256	120	139	178	153	150

No. 14. Bangalore Suryanarain Rao

Birth Details—Born on 12-2-1856 at 12-21 p.m. (L.M.T.) (Lat. 18° 0′ N., Long. 84° 0′ E.).

Planetary Positions—The Sun 301° 12′; the Moon 18° 29′; Mars 180° 53′; Mercury 308° 27′; Jupiter 321° 38′; Venus 260° 33′; Saturn 63° 20′; Rahu 6° 9′; and Ascendant 43° 9′. Ayanamsa 20° 24′. Balance of Venus' Dasa: 12 years, 3 months, 9 days.

Ashtakavarga Figures—The Sun: 4(1), 3, 6(2), 5(2), 3, 3, 5(1), 4, 4(1), 4(1), 4, 3. *The Moon*: 5(1), 2, 4(2), 3, 6(2), 5(2), 4, 5(1), 4, 2, 6(2), 3. *Mars*: 4(3), 3(1), 4(1), 6(4), 1, 2, 3, 4, 4(3), 3(1), 3, 2. *Mercury*: 4(1), 3, 5, 7(4), 3, 3, 5, 3, 6(3), 7(4), 5, 3. *Jupiter*: 4, 8, 2, 2, 7(3), 4(1), 7(5), 6(4), 4, 3, 5(3), 4(2). *Venus*: 4, 2, 5(1), 4(2), 5(1), 6(1), 4, 2, 7(3), 4(2), 4, 5. *Saturn*: 1, 3, 2, 4(1), 4(3), 4(2), 4(2), 4(1), 4(3), 2, 4(2), 3. *Sarvashtakavarga*: 26(6), 24(1), 28(6), 31(13), 29(9), 27(6), 32(8), 28(6), 33(13), 25(8), 31(7), 23(2).

SODYA PINDAS

	Sun	*Moon*	*Mars*	*Mercury*	*Jupiter*	*Venus*	*Saturn*
Rasi Pindas :	52	83	87	70	159	68	115
Graha Pindas :	30	35	41	26	100	26	77
Sodya Pindas :	82	118	128	96	259	94	192

No. 15. Dr. Rabindranath Tagore

Birth Details—Born on 7-5-1861 at 2-51 a.m. (L.M.T.) (Lat. 22° 40′ N., Long. 88° 30′ E.).

Planetary Positions—The Sun 25° 48′ the Moon 351° 59′; Mars 61° 36′; Mercury 9° 18′; Jupiter 117° 24′; Venus 24° 32′; Saturn 132° 37′; Rahu 266° 17′; and Ascendant 336° 9′. Ayanamsa 20° 28′. Balance of Mercury's Dasa : 10 years, 2 months, 20 days.

Ashtakavarga Figures—The Sun : 3, 5(1), 4, 2, 4(1), 4, 2, 3(1), 6, 5(1), 5(1), 5(3). *The Moon*: 3, 3, 5, 4(2), 5(2), 2, 6, 3(1), 4(1), 7(5), 5, 2. *Mars* : 3, 4, 5(5), 1, 5(2), 4, 0, 2(1), 3, 4, 4(4), 4(3). *Mercury* : 6, 3, 7(5), 2, 6, 4, 2, 2, 7, 4(1), 6(1) 5(3). *Jupiter* : 6(2), 4, 3, 7(5), 4, 6(2), 3, 3, 6(2), 8(1), 2, 4(1) 2. *Venus* : 6(3), 6(5), 5(1), 3, 3, 1, 4, 7(3), 3, 3, 6, 5(2). *Saturn*: 2, 5(1), 3(2), 1, 3(1), 2, 3(1), 4(3), 4(2), 5(4), 3, 4(2). *Sarvashtakavarga* : 29(5), 30(7), 32(13), 20(7), 30(6), 23(2), 20(1), 24(9), 33(5), 36(12), 33(7), 27(13).

SODYA PINDAS

	Sun	Moon	Mars	Mercury	Jupiter	Venus	Saturn
Rasi Pindas :	80	70	148	92	78	127	129
Graha Pindas :	20	30	65	55	84	69	31
Sodya Pindas :	100	100	213	147	162	196	160

No. 16. Joseph Stalin

Birth Details—Born on 20/21-12-1879 at 3-5 a.m.(L.M.T.)(Lat. 42° 0′ N., Long. 44° 7′ E.).

Planetary Positions—The Sun 248° 4′; the Moon 344° 10′; Mars 22° 26′; Mercury 229° 10′; Jupiter 316° 30′; Venus 202° 4′: Saturn 348° 20′; Rahu 266° 51′; and Ascendant 194° 44′. Ayanamsa 20° 43′. Balance of Saturn's Dasa : 3 years, 6 months, 26 days.

Ashtakavarga Figures—The Sun : 4, 2, 3(2), 5(3), 4, 5(2), 5(4), 2, 6(2), 6(4), 1, 5(3). *The Moon*: 1, 6(1), 4(3), 4(2), 7(6), 5, 1, 2, 5(4), 6, 5(4), 3(1). *Mars* : 3, 4, 1, 3, 3, 4, 4(3), 3, 3, 5, 2(1), 4(1). *Mercury* : 5, 4, 3(1), 4(1), 5, 3, 7(5), 6(3), 5, 7(4), 2, 3. *Jupiter*: 5(2), [illegible], 7(2), 6(3), 4(1), 3, 6(1), 3, 4, 7(4), 5. *Venus*: 2, 4, 6(2), 5(2), 3(1), 3, 6(2), 6(3), 5(3), 5(2), 4, 3. *Saturn* : 1, 2, 4(2), 5(5), 6(5), 4(2), 3(2), 0, 3(2), 6(4), 1, 4(4). *Sarvashtakavarga*: 21(2), 25(1), 24(10), 33(15), 34(15), 28(5), 29(16), 25(7), 30(11), 39(14), 22(9), 27(9).

SODYA PINDAS

	Sun	Moon	Mars	Mercury	Jupiter	Venus	Saturn
Rasi Pindas :	140	194	44	91	109	109	196
Graha Pindas :	68	70	41	50	61	44	64
Sodya Pindas :	208	264	85	141	170	53	260

No. 17. (R. 183)

Birth Details—Born on 30-10-1903 at 9-30 a.m. (L.M.T.) (Lat. 17° 40′ N., Long. 75° 57′ E.).

Planetary Positions—The Sun 195° 1′; the Moon 310° 23′; Mars 246° 18′; Mercury 181° 35′; Jupiter 322° 81′; Venus 152° 24′; Saturn 292° 6′; Rahu 164° 3′; and Ascendant 70° 36′. Ayanamsa 21° 3′. Balance of Rahu Dasa : 12 years, 11 months, 24 days.

Ashtakavarga Figures—The Sun : 4, 2, 4, 6(2), 6(2), 4(2), 4(1),4, 4, 3(1), 3, 4. *The Moon*: 5, 6(4), 2, 4, 6(1), 2, 2, 5(1),5, 4(2), 4(2). 4. *Mars* : 4, 0, 2, 6(3). 5(1), 2(2), 2, 3, 5(1), 3(3), 3(1), 4. *Mercury* : 3, 2, 4, 7(3), 4(1), 8(6), 4(1), 4, 5(2), 5(3), 3, 5. *Jupiter*: 3, 4, 7(3),5(1), 4(1), 3, 6(2), 4, 6(3), 4(1), 4, 6. *Venus*: 5(1), 5, 5, 2, 5(1), 6(3), 6(2), 4(1), 4, 3, 4, 3(1).*Saturn*: 4(1), 4(2), 4(1), 5(2), 4(2), 3(1), 2, 4(1), 2, 2, 2, 3. *Sarvashtakavarga* : 28(2), 23(6), 28(4), 35(11), 34(9), 28(14), 26(6), 28(3), 31(6), 24(10), 23(3), 29(1).

SODYA PINDAS

	Sun	*Moon*	*Mars*	*Mercury*	*Jupiter*	*Venus*	*Saturn*
Rasi Pindas :	50	90	67	92	84	66	76
Graha Pindas :	29	40	52	83	49	41	7
Sodya Pindas :	79	130	119	175	133	107	83

No. 18. (18/104)

Birth Details—Born on 24-2-1911 at 7-30 a.m. (I.S.T.) (Lat. 20° 28′ N., Long. 85° 54′ E.).

Planetary Positions—The Sun 313° 12′; the Moon 255° 6′; Mars 266° 0′; Mercury 294° 42′; Jupiter 203° 23′; Venus 334° 29′; Saturn 11° 4′; Rahu 22° 25′; and Ascendant 337° 14′. Ayanamsa 21° 8′. Balance of Venus' Dasa : 17 years, 4 months, 16 days.

Ashtakavarga Figures—The Sun : 1, 5(1), 4, 2, 5(4), 5(2), 5(1), 3(1), 5(4), 3, 6(2), 4(2). *The Moon* : 4, 6, 3, 4(3), 6(2), 6(1), 4(1), 3(2), 4, 5, 3, 1. *Mars* : 2, 3, 3, 4(1), 3(1), 2, 4(1), 3, 4(2), 4(2), 3, 4(1). *Mercury* : 3, 5, 5(4), 5(2), 3, 4, 7(6), 3, 5(2), 7(3), 1, 6(3). *Jupiter* : 6(1), 3, 5(2), 4, 6(1), 5(2), 5(3), 5, 5, 6(3), 2, 4. *Venus* : 4, 5(3), 5(1), 5(1), 4, 2, 4, 6(2), 4, 5(3), 4, 4. *Saturn* : 1, 4(2), 3, 0, 6(5), 5(3), 3, 3(3), 3(2), 2, 6(3), 3(3). *Sarvashtakavarga* : 21(1), 31(6), 28(7), 24(7), 33(13), 29(8), 32(12), 26(8), 30(10), 32(11), 25(5), 26(9).

SODYA PINDAS

	Sun	Moon	Mars	Mercury	Jupite	Venus	Saturn
Rasi Pindas :	157	63	62	151	79	73	196
Graha Pindas :	86	10	53	122	5	15	62
Sodya Pindas :	243	73	115	273	1	88	258

No. 19. (11/146)

Birth Details—Born on 5-12-1914 at 7-15 a.m. (I.M.T.) (Lat. 18° 58′ N., Long. 72° 49′ E.).

Planetary Positions—The Sun 230° 5_′; the Moon 76° 44′; Mars 236° 4′ ; Mercury 214° 17′ ; Jupiter 296° 9′; Venus 219° 12′; Saturn (R) 68° 56′ ; Rahu 309° 17′ ; and Ascendant 233° 57′. Ayanamsa 21° 12′. Balance of Rahu Dasa : 4 years, 4 months, 28 days.

Ashtakavarga Figures—The Sun: 5(1), 4(1), 4(1), 4(1), 5(2), 6(1), 3, 4(1), 3, 3, 4(1), 3. *The Moon* : 6(1), 3, 3(1), 3, 8(5), 5(1), 2, 4(1), 3, 6(3), 2, 4(1). *Mars* : 6, 1, 4(2), 0, 4(1), 6(2), 2, 4(4), 3, 4(3), 2, 3(3). *Mercury* : 5, 1, 5(3), 6(1), 4, 7(3), 2, 6(1), 5(1), 4(3), 4, 5. *Jupiter* : 5, 4(1), 2, 6(2), 7(2), 5(3), 3(1), 6(2), 6(1), 2, 6(4), 4. *Venus*: 4(2), 2, 4, 5(2), 4(2), 8(6), 5(1), 3, 2, 6(4), 4, 5(2). *Saturn*: 6, 2, 3(1), 1, 6(4), 5(1), 4(2), 5(4), 2, 2, 2, 1. *Sarvashtakavarga* : 37(4), 17(2), 25(8), 25(6), 38(16), 42(17), 21(4), 32(13), 24(2), 27(13), 24(5), 25(6).

SODYA PINDAS

	Sun	Moon	Mars	Mercury	Jupiter	Venus	Saturn
Rasi Pindas :	73	105	119	75	129	123	99
Graha Pindas :	35	65	150	85	50	40	110
Sodya Pindas :	108	170	269	160	179	163	209

No. 20. (R 163)

Birth Details—Born on 28/29-1-1905 at 5-00 a.m. (I.M.T.)(Lat. 9° 43′ N., Long. 76° 13′ E.).

Planetary Positions—The Sun 287° 20′ ; the Moon 209° 40′ ; Mars 126° 13′ ; Mercury 263° 37′ ; Jupiter 2° 20′ ; Venus 333° 14′ ; Saturn 300° 36′; Rahu 139° 56′; and Ascendant 259° 55′. Ayanamsa 21° 5′. Balance of Jupiter's Dasa : 4 years, 4 months, 24 days.

Ashtakavarga Figures—The Sun : 3, 4, 1, 3, 7(4), 6(4), 5(4), 5(2), 3, 2, 6(5), 3 *The Moon*: 4(1), 2, 5, 7(3), 3, 3, 5(1), 4, 5(2), 2, 4, 5(1).

Mars: 2, 5, 1, 1, 4(2), 3, 6(5), 3(2), 3(1), 3, 5(4), 3(2). *Mercu* : 3, 7(2), 3, 4, 4(1), 5(1), 5(2), 7(3), 4(1), 4(1), 3, 5(1). *Jupiter*:), 4, 4(1), 5(2), 6(3), 3, 5(2), 5, 3, 7(4), 3, 3. *Venus*: 4, 4, 4, 2, 6(2), 3, 5(1), 5(3), 7(3), 4(1), 5(1), 3(1). *Saturn*: 2, 2, 1, 4(2), 6(4), 4(2), 3(2), 2, 4(2), 2, 5(4), 4(2). *Sarvashtakavarga*: 26(6), 28(19(1), 26(7), 36(16), 27(7), 3 (17), 31(10), 29(9), 24(6), 31(14), 2).

SODYA PINDAS

	Sun	*Moon*	*Mars*	*Mercury*	*Jupiter*	*Venus*	*Saturn*
Rasi Pindas :	150	56	148	99	115	106	158
Graha Pindas :	77	40	104	43	96	45	70
Sodya Pindas :	227	96	252	142	211	151	228

No. 21. Lenin

Birth Details—Born on 22-4-18 0 at 9-42 p.m (L.M.T.) (Lat. 54° 17′ N., Long. 48° 26′ E.).

Planetary Positions—The Sun 1 ° 48′; The Moon 282° 46′; Mars 3° 0′; Mercury 22° 2′; Jupiter 35° 2′; Venus 326° 17′; Saturn 247° 46′ (R); Rahu 92° 51′; and Ascendant 217° 54′. Ayanamsa 20° 36′. Balance of Moon's Dasa : 7 years, 11 months, 3 days.

Ashtakavarga Figures—The Sun: 3, 2, 3, 4(3), 4(3), 4, 6(3), 3, 4(1), 7(5), 4(1), 1. *The Moon*: 5(2), 4(2), 5(1), 3, 6(3), 2, 5, 5, 3, 4(2), 4, 3. *Mars*: 3(1), 1, 4(1), 3, 4(2), 5(1), 3, 3, 2, 4(3), 4(1), 3. *Mercury*: 6(1), 2, 5, 2, 5, 5(3), 5, 3. 7(2), 3(1), 6(1), 5(1). *Jupiter*: 5(2), 7(4), 3, 7(4), 3, 3, 3, 7(2), 5(2), 3, 7(4), 3. *Venus*: 3, 2, 4(2), 2, 4(1), 7(2), 2, 4(2), 6, 3(1), 8(6), 7(3). *Saturn*: 4(2), 2, 2, 2, 2, 4(2), 3(1), 4, 2, 5(3), 5(4), 4(2). *Sarvashtakavarga*: 29(8), 20(6), 26(4) 3(7), 28(9), 30(8), 27(4), 29(4), 29(5), 29(15), 38(17), 29(7).

SODYA PINDAS

	Sun	*Moon*	*Mars*	*Mercury*	*Jupiter*	*Venus*	*Saturn*
Rasi Pindas :	108	82	66	80	148	159	114
Graha Pindas :	37	66	40	40	114	47	79
Sodya Pindas :	145	148	106	120	262	206	193

No. 22. The Nizam of Hyderabad

Birth Details—Born on 6-4-1886 at 6-36 p.m. (L.M.T.) (Lat. 17° 30′ N., Long. 78° 30′ E.).

Planetary Positions—The Sun 355° 50′; the Moon 18° 56′; Mars 135° 45′ (R); Mercury 0° 20′; Jupiter 158° 8′; Venus 312° 18′;

Saturn 71° 42′ ; Rahu 144° 2′ ; and Ascendant 181° 50′. Ayanamsa 20° 48′. Balance of Venus' Dasa : 11 years, 7 months, 6 days.

Ashtakavarga Figures—The Sun : 3, 2, 5(4), 4(2), 4(1), 6(4), 1, 2, 4, 7(4), 5(4), 5(3). *The Moon* : 6(1), 3, 5(3), 3(1), 6(1), 4(1), 6(4), 3, 5, 4(1), 2, 2. *Mars* : 1, 2, 5(4), 4(3), 5(4), 5(3), 1, 1, 4(2), 3, 5(4), 3(2). *Mercury* : 5(2), 4, 4(2), 5(1), 5(2), 5(1), 2, 4, 3, 5, 7(5), 5(1). *Jupiter* : 4, 5, 5(1), 4 5(1), 4(1), 6, 6(2), 5, 3, 4, 5(1). *Venus* : 5(1), 4(1), 6(1), 3, 4, 3, 5, 3, 5(1), 5(1), 6(1), 3. *Saturn* : 2, 1, 3, 4(2), 3(1), 3(2), 4(1), 2, 5(1), 6(5), 3, 3(1). *Sarvashtakavarga* : 26(4), 21(1), 33(15), 27(9), 32(10), 30(12), 25(5), 21(2), 31(4), 33(11), 32(14), 26(8).

SODYA PINDAS

	Sun	Moon	Mars	Mercury	Jupiter	Venus	Saturn
Rasi Pindas :	170	83	185	126	51	50	81
Graha Pindas :	111	43	120	96	28	22	33
Sodya Pindas :	281	126	305	222	79	72	114

No. 23. Swami Vivekananda

Birth Details—Born on 12-1-1863 at 6-33 a.m. (L.M.T.) (Lat. 22° 40′ N., Long. 88° 30′ E.).

Planetary Positions—The Sun 270° 52′ ; the Moon 168° 54′ ; Mars 7° 46′ ; Mercury 283° 13′ ; Jupiter 185° 28′ ; Venus 278° 32′ ; Saturn 165° 2′ ; Rahu 233° 41′ ; and Ascendant 267° 31′. Ayanamsa 20° 30′. Balance of Moon's Dasa : 3 years, 3 months, 27 days.

Ashtakavarga Figures—The Sun : 3(1), 4(2), 5, 5(1), 2, 4(2), 5, 5, 4(2), 2, 5, 4. *The Moon* : 3(2), 5, 3, 6(2), 4(3), 5(1), 5(2), 5, 1, 4, 4(1), 4. *Mars* : 2, 5(2), 4, 4, 2, 3(2), 3, 5(1), 3(2), 1, 3, 4. *Mercury*: 4(2) 7(2), 4, 4, 2, 6(2), 5(2), 4, 6(1), 4, 3, 5(1). *Jupiter* : 5(3), 6, 3, 4(1), 4(2), 4, 7(4), 6, 2, 7(3), 5, 3. *Venus* : 4, 5(1), 4(1), 4, 6(2), 4, 3, 5(1), 5(1), 4, 4(1), 4. *Saturn* : 1, 1, 3, 3, 4(3), 4(3), 3, 5(2), 3(2), 3(2), 6(2), 3. *Sarvashtakavarga* : 22(8), 33(7), 26(1), 30(4), 24(10), 30(10), 31(8), 35(4), 24(7), 25(5), 30(4), 27(1).

SODYA PINDAS

	Sun	Moon	Mars	Mercury	Jupiter	Venus	Saturn
Rasi Pindas :	59	82	47	79	88	66	111
Graha Pindas :	28	46	20	56	115	—	64
Sodya Pindas :	87	128	67	135	203	66	175

INDEX OF TECHNICAL TERMS

Aridra	...	6th Constellation—*Orionis*
Ashtakavarga	...	Eight sources of energy, th planets are subjected to.
Ashtakavarga Dasa	...	Directions based on Ashtakavarga
Aslesha	..	9th Constellation—*Hydrae*
Asthangatha	...	Combustion
Ayurdaya	...	Longevity
Bahubhumipala	..	King of many countries
Beejasphuta	...	Procreative power of a male
Bharani	..	2nd Constellation—*Arietis*
Bhava	...	House
Bhinnashtakavarga	...	Individual Ashtakavarga
Bhukti	...	A Directional Measure, sub period
Brahmins	...	Holy and religious people and highest among Hindus
Budha	...	Mercury
Chandra	...	The Moon
Chandra Lagna	...	Sign occupied by the Moon
Chapala Vak	...	Unsteady talk
Chitta	...	14th Constellation—*Virginis Spica*
Dasa	...	Directional Measure, a period
Deekshita	...	Performer of Sacrifice
Dhanus	...	Sagittarius
Dusthana	...	Evil Places (6, 8, 12)
Ekadhipathya Sodhana	...	Reduction on account of a planet owning two signs
Garga	...	A great sage
Gochara	...	Transit Results
Graha Gunakara	...	Planetary Factor
Graha Pinda	...	Product of Bindus and Planetary Factor

Guru ... Jupiter
Horamakaranda ... An ancient Treatise on Astrology
Kakshya ... Orbit—1/8th of a sign
Kanya ... Virgo
Karaka ... Indicator
Kataka ... Cancer
Kendra ... Quadrants
Keraleeya ... An Astrological work
Kesava Paddhathi ... An ancient work on Mathematical Astrology
Kethu ... Cauda
Krittika ... 3rd Constellation—*Tauri Alcyone*
Kshetra Sphuta ... Fertility for Conception
Kuja ... Mars
Kumbha ... Aquarius
Lagna ... Ascendant
Lagnashtakavarga ... Benefic Points contributed by the Ascendant
Makara ... Capricorn
Makha ... 10th Constellation—*Leonis Regulus*
Mantra Sastra ... Science of Sound Vibrations
Maraka ... Death-inflicting Planet
Meena ... Pisces
Mesha ... Aries
Mithuna ... Gemini
Mrigasira ... 5th Constellation—*Orionis*
Nakshatra ... Constellation
Naradeeya ... An ancient astrological work
Navamsa ... 1/9th division of a sign
Neechabhanga ... Cancellation of debilitation
Poorvaphalguni ... 11th Constellation—*Leonis*
Poorvashadha ... 20th Constellation—*Sagittarli*

Prasnamarga	...	An ancient astrological classic
Rahu	...	Caput
Rajayoga	...	Planetary Combinations for Political Success
Rasi	...	Sign
Rasi Gunakara	...	Zodiacal Factor
Ravi	...	The Sun
Rekha	...	Malefic Points in Ashtakavarga
Rekha Ashtakavarga	...	Ashtakavarga of malefic units
Rohini	...	4th Constellation—*Tauri Aldebaran*
Sani	...	Saturn
Sarvashtakavarga	...	Total Ashtakavarga
Satabhisha	...	24th Constellation—*Aquarii*
Simha	...	Leo
Sodya Pinda	...	Sum of the Rasi and Graha Pindas
Sripathi Paddhathi	...	An ancient book on Mathematical Astrology
Sudra	...	Farmer : fourth caste among Hindus
Sukra	...	Venus
Thula	...	Libra
Trikona	...	Trine (1, 5, 9)
Trikona Reductions	...	Reductions in Triangular Signs like Aries, Leo and Sagittarius
Upachaya	...	3, 6, 10, 11 signs
Vaisyas	...	Traders—third caste among Hindus
Vargottama Navamsa	...	A Planet occupying same Rasi and Navamsa
Vedas	..	Teachings
Visakha	...	16th Constellation—*Librae*
Vrischika	...	Scorpio
Vrishabha	...	Taurus
Yugma Navamsa	...	Even Navamsa